History of the Founder of
The Moo Duk Kwan® Organization
Teaching the martial arts style of Soo Bahk Do (Tang Soo Do)
Kwan Jang Nim
Hwang Kee
Nov. 9th 1914 - July 14th, 2002

By
Steven Lemner

(This project would not haven been possible without the guidance and historical input of Kwan Jang Nim H.C. Hwang. Special thanks to Frank Bonsignore, Sa Bom Nim and Roberto Bonefont Sr., Sa Bom Nim for their insights and proof reading, and historical input.)

Kwan Jang Nim Hwang Kee

Founder of

The Moo Duk Kwan® Organization©

In Teaching the Style of Martial arts called: Soo Bahk Do® (Tang Soo Do)

1862 June 13th: Hwang Kees father born Hwang Yong Hwan, Educated in Chinese Classics and History. He attended the Law Academy and held the title of Hoon Mun Gwan (Extensive Literary Scholar) He also held the position of Government Secretary.

Born: Hwang Kee: November 9, 1914 in Jang Dan, Kyong Ki province. (where the DMZ is now) Named Tae Nam (Star Boy), by his father, youngest of three children. One brother 20 years older, and one sister

1914 May 13th: the future Mrs. Hwang Kee was born (Cho Kyung Kap)

1919: Hwang Kee's mother passes away

1921: Exposed to Tae Kyun, Sip Pal Ki at a (Dan Oh festival) (7 yrs old)

1925: Started Elementary school, age 11

1928 April: Married Cho Kyung Kap (though an arranged marriage, typical of the time and culture) They had five children; two boys and three girls. Hwang Hyun Chul was the first son.

1935 March: Graduated High school, age 21 (on track team, abacus team, interest in astronomy)

1936: Began martial arts studies in Manchuria, China, Introduced to Master Yang, Kuk Jin

1936- 1945 Begins work for the Railway Company, Cho Sun Railway Bureau, Jo Yang Chun Station

1937: Returned to Seoul for personal reasons

1940's

1941: Returned to Manchuria, China, to visit and train with Master Yang.

1945: August 15th, World War II ends

1946: China become a Communist country. Hwang Kee is unable to communicate or visit Master Yang

November 9th, 1945: Founded the Moo Duk Kwan organization and established first, Hwa Soo Do class in the Ministry of Transportation, Yong San Ku, Seoul Korea

1947 March 4th: H. C. Hwang (Jin Mun Hwang) Born Seoul, Korea,(the oldest child)

1947 March: Attempted to unify the five major existing organizations in Korea:

A) Moo Duk Kwan

B) Chung Do Kwan

C) Yeun Moo Kwan

D) Song Moo Kwan

E) YMCA Kwon Bup Bu

1947: Presided as chairman at the first Hwa Soo Do demonstration in the Transportation High School Gymnasium

1947 May, 7th Established the first Regional branch Moo Duk Kwan school in Dae Jun City, Choong-Nam Province. Sam Hyun Nam (#4) was appointed as an Instructor

1947, June 5th, Established Moo Duk Kwan school , Teaching Hwa Soo Do (Tang Soo Do) school in the Department of Railways.

1947, July 7th, Established Moo Duk Kwan school , teaching Hwa Soo Do (Tang Soo Do) style in the Labor Department

1948: Arrested and tortured for the first time, in an unsuccessful attempt to force him to confess that he was a left-wing Communist sympathizer. After several days of torture and imprisonment he was released. (This event was precipitated by flyers, that were found on the floor where he taught that supported Communist activities and North Korean political policy. This was believed to be an attempt by a competitor to discredit him and his growing success and visibility of his martial arts organization)

1949, May 30th, Authored the first *Hwa Soo Do Kyo Bohn* textbook in Korea

1949 October 19th, 3rd Hwa Soo Do demonstration at Transportation Technical High School

1950's

1950, June 25th, Korean war begins and suspends teaching for seventeen months

1950 July: Hwang Kee's family relocates to Seok Got Ri. (a village located in the town of Jang Dan Myun, which he was born, to be with family and relatives during these uncertain times)

1950 July: Hwang family's one year old child dies, from the difficult times and conditions

1950: North Koreans begins to investigate the loyalty of employees of the Ministry of Transportation.

1950: Arrested a second time by Communist Party and North Korean military (after all employees are asked to write a biography describing their history, employment, political beliefs and loyalties). He fled to his fathers relative in Seoul, to escape, but was found, arrested, then released, then followed by party officials, and escaped using his martial arts skills, and fled to a cousins home in Tchang Sin Dong, Dong Dae Mun Ku, Seoul.

1950 September: General MacArthur's forces move into Seoul, Hwang Kee returns home

1950: Returns to work at the Ministry of Transportation, and is arrested a third time and tortured in another unsuccessful attempt to make him confess, after a Mr. Kim, found evidence the North Koreans had forced him to write.

1951 January 4th: Hwang Kee and family flees on foot and railroad 146 miles southeast to Dae Gu. It was due t the January 4th Retreat by the North Korea and Chinese forces attack.

1951 June: Arrested a fourth time and accused of sympathizing with North Koreans, he resisted and was severely beaten, tortured by hanging upside down, water boarding, then trying to force him to confess. As he was lead one day by a guard with a rifle and given a blanket (use to wrap dead bodies), he was convinced that he was to be sho the guard said he forgot something and they returned to torture him more. Thinking his family would be shot also he did not confess, he signed a confession. His family was working to free him , and had a relative (Hwang Jin Young, Hwang Kee's older brothers son, who was a prosecutor and carried a high level of authority, and powerful government position) after seeing him demanded his release, and commanded the police to apologize and rewrite their report and repudiate the confession.

1951 October: Hwang Family relocates to Pusan, opens a Moo Duk Kwan organization studio, teaching Tang So (Hwa Soo) Do at the Cho Ryang Station.

1951 November, Established temporary Moo Duk Kwan Headquarters in Cho Ryang-Dong, Pusan

1952 April, Began teaching at the Police Academy in Pusan

1952, October, Began instruction at the Ministry of Defense in Pusan

1953 September, Returned to Seoul to re-establish Moo Duk Kwan Headquarters after Korean War ends.

1953, Established Korean Tang Soo Do Association, presiding as Chairman

1953 November, Established Moo Duk Kwan studios in middle and high schools throughout Korea

1953 December, Applied to join Korean Athletic Association

1954 April, Established a Moo Duk Kwan studio in Mapo Correctional Facility, teaching Tang Soo Do

1954 July, Attempted to unify Korean Tang Soo Do Association and Korean Kong Soo Do Association (Chong D Kwan, Jido Kwan, Chang Moo Kwan, Song Moo Kwan)

1955 May, Grand Opening of Moo Duk Kwan headquarters (43-1 Dong Ja-Dong, Choong Gu, Seoul)

1955 July, Established the following provincial Moo Duk Kwan branches: 1
Seoul: Tchang Young Chung (#15), Se Joon Oh (#26), Seong Heon Chung (#28), Poong Tcheon Kim (17), Hee Seok Choi (#5), Kang Ik Lee (#19), 2) Kyung Ki Do: In Seok Kim (#12), Yong Ha Park (#21), 3) Gang Won, 4) Kyung Buk: Jong Soo Hong (#10), 5) Kyung Nam: Eok Tcheon Lee (#49), 6)Chun Nam, 7) Choong Buk: Sam Hyun Nam (#4), Myong Soon Lim (#20).

1955 August, Ministry of Education prohibits teaching Tang Soo Do in middle and high schools throughout Kore

1955 August, Established a Moo Duk Kwan studio in Seo Dae Moon Correctional Facility, teaching Tang Soo Dc style martial arts.

1955 August, Established a Moo Duk Kwan studio at Korean Air Force Headquarters. Young Tae Han (#37) was appointed as an Instructor, teaching Tang Soo Do.

1955 October 30th: Organized and chaired first International Goodwill Demonstration between Korea and China, at Si Gong Kwan (City Public Hall)

1956: Retires from Ministry of Transportation to focus fulltime on development of the Moo Duk Kwan

1956 March, Begins teaching at Korean Air Force Academy.

1956 March, Dispatched instructors to the following bases: Soo Won: Young Seok Kim(#32), Sa Chun: Myung Kyu Kang (#59), Dae Gu: Sang Seop Ji (#39), and Dae Jun Air Force Academy,

1956 May Begins instructing at Korean Navel Academy. Jin Tae Hwang (#11) was appointed as an Instructor.

1956 June, Established a Moo Duk Kwan studio at Korean Navel Headquarters. Young Taek Kim was appointed (#526)

1956 June, Established a Moo Duk Kwan studio , teaching a Tang Soo Do Style of martial arts at In Ha Engineering University. Young Ha Park (#21)

1956 October, Established a Moo Duk Kwan studio, teaching Tang Soo Do, at Korean Military Police Headquarters

1956 October, Established a Moo Duk Kwan studio at Army Printing Corps, teaching Tang Soo Do style

1956 November, Established a Moo Duk Kwan studio at the R.O.K. 2nd Army, teaching Tang Soo Do style

1957: Introduced to the *Moo Yei Do Bo Tong Ji,* at Seoul National Library, by Professor Na Hyun Seong of the Seoul National University

1957 Dale Drouillard (#757) becomes 1st American serviceman to achieve Dan under Hwang Kee, through the Moo Duk Kwan organization, teaching Tang Soo Do style of martial arts.

1957 May 18th, Taught Tang Soo Do at Seoul Technical High School

1957 May, Established a Moo Duk Kwan studio ,at Korean Marine Corps. Teaching Tang Soo Do style of martial arts. Soo Yong Cha (#269)

1957 July, Established a Moo Duk Kwan studio at Han Yang University in Seoul. Teaching Tang Soo Do style of martial arts. Hee Seok Choi (#5)

1957 September, Established Moo Duk Kwan studio at the U.S. 8th Army in Young San. Teaching Tang Soo Do style of martial arts. Sang Kyu Shim (#180)

1958 July, Authored second Tang Soo Do self-defense textbook (Tang Soo Do Bo Sin Bop)

1958 November 30th: International Goodwill Demonstration with Korea, China and USA, Seoul, Korea

1959 May, Established Moo Duk Kwan studio in Seoul Agricultural University in Soo Won. Teaching Tang Soo Do style of martial arts. Young Hwan Lee (#147)

1959 July, Established Moo Duk Kwan studio in Koryo University, Seoul. Teaching Tang Soo Do style of martial arts. Jin Gil Kim (#99).

1959 October, Established Moo Duk Kwan studio at Air Force University. Teaching Tang Soo Do style of martial arts. Nak Eon Baek (#194).

1959: Mariano Estioko (#759) becomes second American to achieve Dan under Hwang Kee's Moo Duk Kwan organization.

1960's

1960 June, Authored Tang Soo Do self-defense textbook

1960 June, Created name "Soo Bahk Do" from ancient name of Soo Bahk, Soo Bahk Ki, or Soo Bahk Hee

1960 June 30th, Moo Duk Kwan and Ji Do Kwan organizations were joined as the Korean Soo Bahk Do Association, headed by Kwan Jang Nim Hwang Kee

1960 September, Published Moo Yei Si Bo (Martial Arts Newspaper)

1960 June 30th: Using ancient Korean martial arts name, incorporated and registered with the Korean Ministry o Education under the name of Dae Han Soo Bahk Do Hoe (Korean Soo Bahk Do Association) becoming the first member association

1960-1962: Returning servicemen and others begin opening Tang Soo Do studios in U.S. including:

Dale Drouilard (#757) in Wyandotte, Michigan / Robert Thompson(#1791) in Dayton Ohio / Lawrence Seiberlich(#1815) in St. Paul Min. / John Butterwick(#2277)Military / Robert Cheezic (#2278) Waterbury, CT. Carlos 'Chuck' Norris (#2819),Torrance Ca. / Frank Trojanowicz (#13333) / Joe Weeks(#3596),Magnolia Ar. Lynn Jackson(#3597) Oberlin, Ohio / James Ruston(#4130) Military / Russell Hanke(#4137)Detroit Mich. Robert Sohn (#6037) New York. / James Cummings(#4493)Military / Robert Shipley(#4825), Honolulu Hi David J. Praim(#3593), Mt. Clemems, MI, / Robert Beaudoin (#5657) Waterbury, CT. / Jong Hyan Lee (#1885), San Dieg Ca. / Lynn Jackson (#3597) , Lorain Ohio / Ki Whang Kim (No Dan Bon) (Washington D.C.) / Shim Sang Kyu(#180) Wyandotte, Mi. / Ahn Kyong Won (#1763) Cincinnati, OH

1960 July: Ji Do Kwan becomes second member to join Korean Soo Bahk Do Association Moo Duk Kwan

1960 October: Instructors assigned to the following USA 8th Army branch studios: 8th Army Headquarters; Moo San: Kyu Sik Shin (#724), Dong Do Chun; Kyong Won Ahn (#1763) ; Inchon; Pusan: Jong Ha Lee (#2002).

1961 May 14th: Formed the Asian Tang Soo Do Association among Korea, Japan and Taiwan

1961: Col. John T. Butterwick (#2277) put in charge of the first U.S. Tang Soo Do Moo Duk Kwan organization b Hwang Kee's Moo Duk Kwan organization.

1961 May 16th: Military Revolution lead by Lt. General Park, Chong Hee begins.

1961-1965: Lt. General Park, Chong Hee and Korean Government forced Hwang Kee to stop the monthly publication of the Moo Yei Si Bo (Martial Arts Newspaper) and also released him as an instructor at the ROK Academy and National Police Academy with no reason. Both lead efforts to dissolve the Korean Soo Bahk Do Association, Moo Duk Kwan, and impede Hwang Kee's activities.

1961 June: Established Chun Buk Province regional branch of the Moo Duk Kwan organization.

1961 June: Established Moo Duk Kwan studio at Hong Ik University, teaching Tang Soo Do style of martial arts.

1961 October: Established a Moo Duk Kwan organization in Michigan, USA.

1962 May: Established Tang Soo Do Association in USA

1962 May: Established a Moo Duk Kwan organization in France

1962 September: Re-registered Korean Soo Bahk Do Association due to ruling of new government

1962 September: Established Moo Duk Kwan organization / Association in Canada

1963: Ki Whang Kim comes to US (Washington D.C.) as Chairmen of Tang Soo Do Moo Duk Kwan in US appointed by Hwang Kee through the Moo Duk Kwan organization.

1963 July: Established Tang Soo Do Association in England

1964: Shim Sang Kyu (#180) official representative of Tang Soo Do Moo Duk Kwan in U.S. sponsored by Russell Hanke (#4137) to come to U.S. to the Detroit area

1964: Participated with Korean team in first Asian Tang Soo Do championship in Japan

1964 July: Established Moo Duk Kwan studio at Yeun Sae University, teaching Tang Soo Do style of martial arts.

1964 November: Established West German Tang Soo Do Association

1964 December: Board of Directors of Soo Bahk Do changed and registered with government

1964 December: Moo Duk Kwan announces revised charter and bylaws

1965: Sponsored and organized Asian Tang Soo Do Championship

1965 January: Established Moo Duk Kwan organization branches in Washington D.C., New York, Michigan, California, Washington, Texas and Florida.

1965-1979: Efforts to dissolve the Moo Duk Kwan and unify with Tae Kwon Do, by Lt. General Choi, Hong He and Korean Government .

These include some of the following actions:

A. Impediments to acquire passports/ visa's to travel to teach Soo Bahk Do

B. Political pressure on Moo Duk Kwan instructors to leave the Moo Duk Kwan and join

Tae Kwon Do. (rank, materials, and political status)

C. Attempts to destroy organizations record of rank and seniority.

D. revoking the registration and recognition of the same Korean Soo Bahk Do Association,

Moo Duk Kwan

E. Prohibited from attending international events

1965 May: Korean Soo Bahk Do Association's Legal status revoked; decision appealed to appellate level and reli granted.

1965 August: Established a Moo Duk Kwan organization in the Philippines. Casimiro Grandeza (#2883) teaching Tang Soo Do.

1965 December 28th : Korean Government appeals appellate decision to Supreme Court, won the judgment

1966 Dr. Robert Sohn (#6037) forms the N.Y Moo Duk Kwan Association. He with Edward Gross (#6780), Vincent Nuno (#7291) were put in charge by Grandmaster Hwang Kee to oversee teaching and promotions in the N.Y area.

1966 June 21st : Korean Government rules in favor of Korean Soo Bahk Do Association

1966 November: Revised Moo Duk Kwan regulations

1966 December: Revised charter and by-laws of Korean Soo Bahk Do Association as required by the Korean Government

1967: Established Moo Duk Kwan in Malaysia. Hwa Yong Chung (#410), Soon Ho Chang (#3722). teaching Tan Soo Do.

1968: Established a Moo Duk Kwan organization in Italy

1968: Sponsored and organized first World and fifth Asian Tang Soo Do Championship at Citizen Hall, Seoul

1968 August: Election of new Korean Soo Bahk Do Association Board of Directors and registration with government.

1968: Established a Moo Duk Kwan organization in Greece. George R. Page (#11772) teaching Tang Soo Do.

1969: Participated at the second World and sixth Asian Tang Soo Do Championship (Philippines)

1970's

1970 April : Published Soo Bahk Do Dae Kham (Korean Version)

1973: Awarded "Da Ma Roo" from Philippines President Marcos

1973 May: Dispatched HC Hwang (DB509) to Greece

1974 March: Established a Moo Duk Kwan organization in Belgium (Instructor: Beom Ju Lee #11870) teaching Tang Soo Do.

1974 October: United States Soo Bahk Do Moo Duk Kwan directors convention and general meeting of all USA members at Burlington, NJ

The Task Force Members were: (Sa Boms /Masters and other) 1. Jae Chul Shin (#698) 2. Robert Thompson(#1791) 3. Tchang Bok Chung (#12641) 4. Chuck Blackburn (#12197) 5. Arthur Fontaine (#14350) 6. Joe Weeks (#3696) 7. Andy Ahpo (#10187), and Charles di Pierro.

Officers of the first Board of Directors, of the U.S. Tang Soo Do Moo Duk Kwan Federation™ were:

Kwan Jang Nim Hwang Kee, President

Hyun Chul Hwang(#509) TAC Chairman, Charles di Pierro, Chairman of Board, Victor Martinov (#10189), Vice Chairman of Board,

Andy Ah Po (#10187), Secretary , Arthur Pryor (16505) , Treasurer

additional members of the board were: Chun Sik Kim (#2457) , Russ Hanke (#4137), Frank Trojanowicz (#13333), Robert Shipley (#4825), Lynn Jackson (#3597) , Robert Kingsley (#6044), Tchang-Bok Chung (#12641), Joe Weeks (#3596), Larry Seiberlich (#1815), Jeff Moonitz (#17650), Fred Kenyon (#14345), Bob Beaudoin (#5661), Ben Cortese (#11689), Frank Bonsignore (#15805), Dennis Miller (#18430), Ronald Savage (#15879), Lyn Stanwich, James Lee (#14317)

1975 June 28th: United States Soo Bahk Do Charter convention and special seminar by Grandmaster Hwang Kee (Hilton Hotel, NY)

The Charter was ratified making this event the official birth of the Federation.

Those in attendance were: (Sa Boms/Masters/Dans)

Kwan Jang Nim Hwang, Kee, Hyun Chul Hwang (#509), Chun Sik Kim (#2457), Yong Ki Hong (#4142), Andy Ah Po (#10187), Carl Jenkins (#18983), Ronald Savage (#15879), Dennis E. Miller (#18430), Peter Canciani (#18911), Warren Adams, Jeff Moonitz (#17650), Frank Trojanowicz (#13333), Paul Johnson, Frank Bonsignore (#15805), Arthur Pryor (#16505), Benjamin Cortese (#11689), Larry Seiberlich (#1815), Robert Fernandez, Jr. (#17927), Robert Fernandez, Sr. (#14464), Joe Weeks (#3596), Ki Yul Yu (#5311), Holly A. Whitehouse (#18943), James N. Rushton, Victor Martinov (#10189), Fred Kenyon (#14345), Joyce M. Keyes (#19448), Russell Hanke (#4137), Robert Beaudoin (#5661), Robert Rondelli (#17416), Psyche Harry Smith (#18143), James Lee (#14317), Greg William (#11695), Robert Shipley (#4825)

1974 November: Participated in first Pan-Hellenic Martial Arts Championship in Athens, Greece

1976 October: Each foreign branch holds Soo Bahk Do meeting and convention

1977 January 19th: Korean Tae Kwon Do Association established a policy to eliminate the traditional and histo names of the Kwan's. and to identify them by number.

1977 May: Organized and conducted special National Tang Soo Do Moo Duk Kwan Championship at Concord Hotel, Monticello, NY

1977: Developed the Il Soo Sik standardization

1978: Developed the Ho Sin Sool standardization

1978 October: 3rd World Soo Bahk Do Moo Duk Kwan Championship at London, England

1978 November 9th: Hwang Kee turns 64

1980's

1980 July: Sponsored and participated in World Ko Dan Ja meeting in Newark , NJ

1980 December: Sponsored and organized Goodwill Soo Bahk Do Moo Duk Kwan Championships between Kor and USA held at Jang Choong Gym, Seoul

1981 September: Sponsored and participated in World Ko Dan Ja meeting, regarding 1982 World Championship in Atlantic City, NJ

1982 May: Special Soo Bahk Do Moo Duk Kwan seminar and clinic held at U.S. Air Force Academy, Colorado

1982 November 4th: International and fourth United States National Tang Soo Do Moo Duk Kwan Championshi at Atlantic City, NJ. during which Hwang Kee presented the first public presentation of material translated from th Moo Yei Do Bo Tong Ji (Hwa Sung Hyung)

1982 December: England national Soo Bahk Do Championship

1983: August: Sponsored and organized special Chil Sung Hyung seminar and clinic

1983 December; Organized and attended the *FIRST week long Ko Dan Ja testing,* Springfield, NJ

1984 October: 6th United States Tang Soo Do Moo Duk Kwan Championship at West Point Military Academy Gym, NY

1984: Developed the Tanto standardization

1984 November: All England National Soo Bahk Do Moo Duk Kwan Championship

1984 November: Special Chil Sung Clinic for European region at London , England

1985: Developed the Bong standardization

1985 March: Attended special Chil Sung Clinic for the South East Asia region at Sarawak, Malaysia

1987 July: Special International Summer Camp Training at Pathwork Center, NY

1987 December: Attended special Chil Sung Hyung Clinic for South America at Buenos Aires, Argentina

1988 March: Organized special clinic for European region at Athens, Greece

1988 May: Grand opening ceremony for new building for World Moo Duk Kwan Headquarters, Seoul, Korea

1988: Special clinic and Ko Dan Ja meeting for Southeast Asia region at Kuala Lumpur, Malaysia

1988 November: Attended Tenth United States Tang Soo Do Moo Duk Kwan Championship at West Point, NY

1988 December: Sponsored and organized World Ko Dan Ja special training in Seoul, Korea

1989 January: Attended Ko Dan Ja meeting and initiates discussion of "Mission 2000" agenda

1989 March: Opening of new Headquarters for the Korean Soo Bahk Do Association, Seoul, Korea

1989 May 15th: Sponsored and attended International Soo Bahk Do Goodwill Demonstration and clinics at the Lotte Hotel in Seoul, Korea

1989: Black Belt Magazines "Man of the Year"

1990's

1990 January: announces "Mission 2000", along with long range plan for the future of the Moo Duk Kwan

1990 March: Conducted International Seminar, London, England

1990 March: Conducted National Clinics in Belgium, Italy, and Greece

1990 April: Organized special Ko Dan Ja meeting of Korean Soo Bahk Do Association Moo Duk Kwan in Seoul, Korea

1991 March: Conducted the FIRST Yuk Ro clinics presenting material and movements translated form the *Moo Yei Do Bo Tong Ji*

1991 December: International demonstration and clinic, Mar Del Plata, Argentina

1992 March: Published 424 pages of Soo Bahk Do (Korean Version) describing the Yuk Ro movements form the Moo Yei Do Bo Tong Ji.

1992 March: Conducted Yuk Ro and Chil Sung Hyung clinics, Headquarters, Seoul, Korea

1992 June: Attended the International Demonstration and Clinics at Athens, Greece

1992 November: Published Soo Bahk Do (Tang Soo Do) Volume II (English Version)

1993: Presented an award for "his Contributions to better human relations" by the New York Korean Association

1993 April: Conducted the annual European clinic, Bruxelles, Belgium

1993 June: Published History of Moo Duk Kwan (Korean Version)

1993 August; Published Moo Do Chul Hahk (Korean Version)

1993 August: Published Instructional Guides for Soo Bahk Do Moo Duk Kwan (4 Volumes)

1993 November: The 1st Youth Soo Bahk Do Moo Duk Kwan Goodwill Championship, Zurich, Switzerland

1994 February: Official announcement of the Moo Duk Kwan 50th Anniversary event in Seoul, Korea

1994 June: Annual European Clinic and meeting for preparing the European Soo Bahk Do Moo Duk Kwan Federation, Bruxelles, Belgium

1994 September: International Youth Goodwill Championship, Zurich, Switzerland

1994 September: Official birth of the European Soo Bahk Do Moo Duk Kwan Federation, Zurich, Switzerland

1994 October: Appointed Task force member for future Mexican National Moo Duk Kwan Federation

1994 October: Last time Hwang Kee attends the Ko Dan Ja, in the United States

1994 December: Published Limited Edition for the Instructional Guides (Hard cover, all four volumes)

1995 January: Sponsored Technical Advisory Committee meeting, San Diego, California

1995 April: 1st European Soo Bahk Do Moo Duk Kwan Federation Clinic and meeting

1995: History of the Moo Duk Kwan (English Version)

1995 September: 50th Anniversary Celebration of the Moo Duk Kwan, Seoul, Korea Culture and Educational Center, Seoul, Korea

1996 August 3rd: The U.S. Tang Soo Do Moo Duk Kwan Federation Inc. changed it's name to the U.S. Soo Bahk Do Moo Duk Kwan Federation Inc.

1997 October 14th: Mrs. Hwang Kee, Cho Kyung Kap passes away at the age of 83 (married to Hwang Kee for [illegible] years)

2000's

2000 October: 55th Anniversary Celebration of the Moo Duk Kwan. -Millennium visit to Seoul, Korea for Hwang Kee from World wide.

2000: 1st Moment with the Masters held with Ko Dan Ja testing

2002 October: 1st Korean Ko Dan Ja week long Testing at Dae Doon Mountain.

2002 July 14th: Hwang Kee passes away. (88/89 yrs old **depending on Korean birth traditions)

2005: 60th Anniversary Celebration of the Moo Duk Kwan, Seoul, Korea

History of Kwan Jang Nim H.C. Hwang
Heir to
Soo Bahk Do (Tang Soo Do) Moo Duk Kwan

Kwan Jang Nim of Soo Bahk Do Moo Duk Kwan
H.C. (Hyun Chul) Hwang
Dan Bon#509

1940's

March 4th, 1947 Born Seoul, Korea,(Birth Name: Jin Mun, the second child of five)

1950's

1953 October 26th: Se Hun (Hwang) was born in Yong San Ku, Korea. (future Mrs. H.C. Hwang) They will meet in 1988, New York City, NY.

1954 May 5th: Entering the Moo Duk Kwan Discipline. (7 years old)

1957 October 27th: Promoted to Cho Dan (1st Dan) in the Moo Duk Kwan

(he was the youngest Dan holder at the time in Korea)

1958 October 19th: Promoted to E Dan (2nd Dan)

1959 March: Graduated from Yong San Elementary School

1960's

1961 October 8th: Promoted to Samdan (3rd Dan)

1962 March: Graduated from Sun Rin Middle School

1965 March: Graduated from Yang Jong High School

1965 November 15th: Promoted to Sa Dan (4th Dan) in the Moo Duk Kwan

1966: Member of the Korean Team at the 5th Asian Karate Championship, held in Seoul ,Korea

1969 September: Graduated from the Korean University (Major in Philosophy) also held a great interest in art illustration.

1970's

1970 May 24th,: Promoted to O Dan (5th Dan) and Sa Bom in the Moo Duk Kwan

Head Technical Advisor for the first World Karate Tournament in Tokyo, Japan

1970-1973: Served as head instructor at the Central Moo Duk Kwan Do Jang and at the U.S. Army base in Yong San

1973 May-1974 June: Served as Head Instructor of the Greek Tang Soo Do Moo Duk Kwan Federation

1973 November: Head official at the first Pan-Hellenic Martial Arts Championship in Athens, Greece

1974 June: Invitational Instructor of the United Kingdom Tang Soo Do Moo Duk Kwan Federation

July 1974: Promoted to Yuk Dan in Soo Bahk Do Moo Duk Kwan.

1974-1975 Moved to United States of America and Opened first Dojang in Springfield, New Jersey.

June 30th, 1975 - July 2002: Serves as the Chairman of the Technical Advisory Committee of the U.S. Soo Bahk Do Moo Duk Kwan Federation (Formerly known as the U.S. Tang Soo Do Moo Duk Kwan Federation)

1978 July, 22nd: The first U.S. Tang Soo Do Moo Duk Kwan Championships, Concord Hotel, NY

1978 October 26th-28th: The 3rd Soo Bahk Do Moo Duk Kwan Championships at London, England. Attended with the U.S. Team members

October 26-28, 1979: U.S. National Convention for Ho Sin Sool / Hyungs standardization

1980's

1980: November: 2nd U.S. Tang Soo Do Moo Duk Kwan Championship, Pittsburg, PA.

1981 April: 3rd U.S. Tang Soo Do Moo Duk Kwan Championship , Roselle Park High School, NJ.

May 1981: Promoted to Chil Dan in Soo Bahk Do Moo Duk Kwan.

1982 November: 4th U.S. Tang Soo Do Moo Duk Kwan Championship / Internationals, Atlantic City, NJ.

1982 November: Attended the special Chil Song Hyung clinic by the founder.

1983 August: The 2nd Chil Song Hyung clinic by the founder. Kang Uk Lee (70), W.Y. Chung(410), C.I. Kim (475), H.C. Hwang (509), and C.S.Kim (2457) were attended.

1983 November: Attended 5th, U.S. Tang Soo Do Moo Duk Kwan Championship, San Diego, CA.

1983 December 4th-7th: The 1st U.S. Ko Dan Ja Shim Sa (for 4 days) at Springfield, NJ. Candidates were; Lloy Francis (14500), Larry Jones (158490, Ron Cehner (18450), Patrick Jorgensen (18934), Daniel Nolan (19035), ar Russ Hanke (4137) as an official.

1984 October: Attended 6th U.S. Tang Soo Do Moo Duk Kwan Championship, West Point, NY

1984 November: Assist at the Founder's Euro Chil Song Hyung clinic in England

1984 December 3rd-7th: The 2nd U.S. Ko Dan Ja Shim Sa at the Springfield HQ Do Jang in NJ. Candidates wer L Seiberlich (1815), Ben Cortese (11689), Jeff Moonitz (17650), Fred Scott (19187), and Russ Hanke (4137) as a official.

1985 May: Assisted at the 2nd Euro Chil Song Hyung Clinic by the founder at the London, England

1985 November: 7th U.S. Tang Soo Do Moo Duk Kwan Championship, Anaheim, CA.

1986 March: Assisted at the 3rd Euro Chil Song Hyung Clinic at London, England

1986 June 13th: Their first daughter is born (Sun Hee Hwang)

1986 August: The 5th World Soo Bahk Do Moo Duk Kwan Championships at the Watford Leisure Center, England.

November 1986: The 3rd U.S. Ko Dan Ja Shim Sa at Springfield HQ Do Jang in NJ. It was the first full 8 days of Shim Sa at the new headquarters Do Jang in NJ. Candidates were; Andy Ahpo (10187), Victor Martinov (10189) Wilton Bennett, Jr. (19027), Frank Schermerhorn (19787), Don Southerton (19192), Charlie Ferraro (19986), Yec Seo (20564), Philip Bartolacci (20571), and Russ Hanke (4137

1986 November: The 8th U.S. Tang Soo Do Moo Duk Kwan Championship , Stamford CN.

1987 June: Assisted the Founder's Chil Song Hyung clinics for the South East Asian Region at Sarawak, Malaysia.

1987 July: International Summer Camp at the Pathwalk Center, NY

1987 November: The 4th U.S. Ko Dan Ja Shim Sa at the headquarters Do Jang, Springfield, NJ

1987 November: The 9th U.S. Tang Soo Do Moo Duk Kwan Championship, Bal Harbor, FL.

1987 December: Assisted the Founder's Chil Song Hyung clinics for the South America Region in Buenos Aires, Argentina.

1988 May: Attended the Grand Opening ceremony for the Central Headquarters Do Jang in Seoul, Korea

1988 July: International Summer Camp at the Pathwalk Center in NY

1988 November: The 5th Ko Dan Ja Shim Sa, U.S.A. , at headquarters Dojang, Springfield, NJ.

1988 November: The 10th U.S. Tang Soo Do Moo Duk Kwan Championship, West Point, NY

1988 December: Assisted the Founder's Ko Dan Ja clinic in Seoul, Korea

1988: Conducted seminars at Winter Camp, (Yuk Ro Hyung) Homestead, FL.

1989 - July 2002: Served as the Vice President for the World Moo Duk Kwan

1989 May15th: Organized the International Goodwill Demonstration & Clinics at the Lotte Hotel in Seoul, Korea.

1989 May: Promoted to Pal Dan in Soo Bahk Do Moo Duk Kwan.

1989 July : International Summer Camp at the Pathwalk Center, NY

1989 October: The 6th Ko Dan Ja Shim Sa, U.S.A. at the Headquarters Dojang, Springfield, NJ.

1989 October: Attended 11th U.S. Tang Soo Do Moo Duk Kwan Championship, Anaheim, CA.

1990's

1990 March: Conduct the Euro Tour for clinics at England, Belgium, Italy, and Greece

1990 April: Assisted the Founder's clinics and meeting with Ko Dan Jas in Korea.

1990 July: International Summer Camp at the Pathwalk Center, NY

1990 October 6th: H.C. Hwang and Se Hun are married

1990 October: The 12th U.S. Tang Soo Do Moo Duk Kwan Championship, Concord Hotel

1990 November: The 7th Ko Dan Ja Shim Sa, U.S.A. at headquarters Do Jang ,Springfield, NJ.

1991 March: The first U.S. TAC Committee members were appointed by the Founder. They were;

W.Y. Chung (410)

L. Seiberlich (1810)

Russ Hanke (4137)

S.D. Cho (8013),

Y.K. Hong (9193),

A. Ahpo (10187),

V. Martinov (10189)

1991 March: Assisted the founder at the 1st Yuk Ro Hyung clinic for newly appointed U.S. TAC members at the headquarters Do Jang in Springfield, NJ

1991 July: Yuk Ro Hyung Clinics for the U.S. Regional Examiners at the Summer Camp at Owaisa Bauer, FL.

1991 August 21st: Their second daughter is born (Ji Min Hwang)

1991 August: International Summer Camp at the Pathwalk Center, NY

1991 November: The 8th Ko Dan Ja Shim Sa, U.S.A. at headquarters Do Jang, Springfield, NJ.

1991 November: The 13th U.S. Tang Soo Do Moo Duk Kwan Championship, Hollywood, FL.

1991 December: Attended and assisted the Founder at the International Demonstration and Clinics in Mar Del Plata, Argentina.

1992 March: Assisted the Founder at the Yuk Ro / Chil Song Hyung Clinic at the Central Headquarters Do Jang Seoul, Korea.

1992 June: Assisted the Founder for the Yuk Ro Hyung Clinics and attended with the U.S. Team for the International Demonstration in Athens, Greece.

1992 July: International Summer Camp at the Pathwalk Center, NY

1992 September: The U.S. Summer Camp in San Bernardino Mountain, CA

1992 October: The 14th U.S. Tang Soo Do Moo Duk Kwan Championship, Ft. Lauderdale, FL.

1992 November: The 9th Ko Dan Ja Shim Sa, U.S.A. at headquarters Dojang ,Springfield, NJ.

1993 April: Attended the Euro Clinic in Bruxelle, Belgium.

1993 July: International Summer Camp in Connecticut.

1993 September: Co-author of the Instructional Guide for Soo Bahk Do Moo Duk Kwan.

1993 October: The 15th U.S. Nationals, Dallas TX.

1993 November: The 10th U.S. Ko Dan Ja Shim Sa at the Headquarters Do Jang in Springfield

1994 January 10th: Their third daughter is born (Ji Sun Hwang)

1994: "Instructional Guides" National Tour, to promote New Gup Instructional Guide books to membership for increased standardization.

1994 June: The annual Euro clinics and meeting for preparing the Euro Federation in Bruxelle, Belgium.

1994 June: International Summer Camp at the Pathwalk Center, NY

1994 September: The 16th U.S. Nationals, San Diego, Ca. The official name changes to the United States Soo Bahk Do Moo Duk Kwan Federation from the United State Tang Soo Do Moo Duk Kwan Federation at this event

1994 September: Attended the 2nd International Youth Goodwill Championships in Zurich, Switzerland.

1994 September: Assisted Birth of the Euro Federation in Zurich, Switzerland.

1994 October: Worked with Mexican Task Force members for the Mexican Soo Bahk Do Moo Duk Kwan Federation.

1994 November: The11th Ko Dan Ja Shim Sa, U.S.A. ,Springfield, NJ. (last time the Founder, Kwan Jang Nim Hwang Kee attended a Ko Dan Ja in the U.S.A.)

1995 April: Attended the 1st Euro Soo Bahk Do Moo Duk Kwan Federation Clinics and meeting since its official birth in Bruxelle, Belgium.

1995 June: The 17th U.S. Nationals, Orlando, FL.

1995 July: International Summer Camp at the Pathwalk Center, NY

1995 September: The Moo Duk Kwan 50th Anniversary Celebration at the Seoul Culture and Educational Center in Seoul, Korea

1995 November: The 12th Ko Dan Ja Shim Sa, U.S.A. at headquarters Dojang, ,Springfield, NJ.

1996 February 24th: Attended and assisted the 1st Euro Soo Bahk Do Moo Duk Kwan Championships at the Nescot Sports Center, Surrey, England.

1996 March 8th: Assisted the Founder the Ko Dan Ja / Instructor's clinic at the Central Do Jang in Seoul, Korea.

1996 March 23rd: Conducted the Euro Spring Camp in Belgium.

1996 May 18th: Reunion with the Mexican Moo Duk Kwan. Conducted clinics and meeting in Mexico City and Queretaro, Mexico.

1996 June 22nd: Conducted Clinics and Demonstration for the French Moo Duk Kwan in Paris, France.

1996 July 18-20: International Summer Camp at the Pathwalk Center in Phoenicia, NY

1996 August 1st-3rd: The 18th U.S. Nationals at the Town & Country Hotel in San Diego, CA.

1996 September 22nd: Assisted the Founder for the Ko Dan Ja / Instructor's Clinic in Seoul, Korea.

1996 October 11th-13th: The U.S. National Camp at the Camp Fern in Marshall, Texas.

1996 October 24th-27th: Conducted the International Goodwill demonstration and clinics in Mendoza, Argentina.

1996 November 10th: Assisted the Canadian Soo Bahk Do Moo Duk Kwan Federation was formed in Toronto, Canada.

1996 November 16th-24th: The 14th U.S. Ko Dan Ja Shim Sa in, at headquarters Dojang, Springfield, NJ

1997 March 29th: Assisted the Founder's Neh Gong Clinic at the Central Do Jang in Seoul, Korea.

1997 April 12th-13th: Conducted the annual Euro Clinic in Belgium. Attended the Grand Opening of the new Headquarters Do Jang for the Belgium Moo Duk Kwan in Perwez, Belgium.

1997 May 17th: Assisted the Founder's Neh Gong Clinics at the Central Do Jang in Seoul, Korea.

1997 July 17th-19th: Conducted clinic for the Mexico Moo Duk Kwan in Mexico City, Mexico.

1997 August 15th: The 19th U.S. Nationals at the Hilton Hotel in Cherry Hill, NJ. Demonstrated Chil Song Yuk Ro Hyung for the first time.

1997 September 12th-13th: Attended the 2nd Euro Soo Bahk Do Moo Duk Kwan Championships in Wald, Switzerland.

1997 October 10th-12th: The U.S. National Camp at the Camp Fern in Marshall, Texas.

1997 October 14th: Mother: Cho Kyung Kap passes away at the age of 83 (married to Hwang Kee for 69 years)

1997 November 15th-23rd: The 15th U.S. Ko Dan Ja Shim Sa at headquarters Dojang, Springfield, NJ

1997 December 6th: Conducted a clinic for the Puerto Rico Moo Duk Kwan in San Juan, P.R..

1997 December 11th-15th: Conducted clinics and demonstration for the 30th years of Moo Duk Kwan in Malaysia at Miri, Sarawak, Malaysia.

1997 December 17th-21st: The first visit to Philippines Moo Duk Kwan and conducted clinics at Davao City. Philippines. Accompanied by Daymon Kenyon (19839), Robert Hedges (22420), and Russell Colston

1998 March 21st-22nd: Assisted the Founder's clinic for Ko Dan Ja and Instructors in Seoul, Korea.

1998 March 28th-29th: Conducted clinics for the Mexico Moo Duk Kwan in Mexico City, Mexico.

1998 April 24th-26th, Conducted the annual Euro Clinics in Belgium.

1998 May 29th-31st: Conducted the U.S National clinics for Chil Song / Yuk Ro Hyung in San Diego, CA

1998 June 13th-14th: Assisted the Founder for the Ko Dan Ja Clinics at the Central Do Jang in Seoul, Korea.

1998 June 26th-28th: International Summer Camp at the Pathwalk Center in Phoenicia, NY

1998 July 14th-17th: Attended and assisted for producing the Study Guide Video.

1998 July 30th-August 1st: The 20th U.S. Nationals, Cincinnati, OH.

1998 August 8th-15th: Conducted the Euro Swiss Camp at the Piz Beverin in Swiss Alps.

1998 August 28th-30th: Conducted Chil Song Yuk Ro Hyung clinic in Seattle, WA.

1998 September 19th-20th: Assisted the Founder for the Ko Dan Ja Clinics at the Central Do Jang in Seoul.

1998 October 9th-11th: The U.S. National Camp at the Camp Fern in Marshall, TX.

1998 November 14th-21st: The 16th U.S. Ko Dan Ja Shim Sa in Highfall, NY (It is the first time having the Ko Dan Ja Shim Sa outside of the Headquarters Do Jang)

1998 December 10th-15th: Conducted the 1st South East Asia Leaderships Seminars (SEALS) in Miri, Sarawak, Malaysia.

1998 December 18th-19th: Assisted the Founder's Clinics for the Ko Dan Ja in Central Do Jang in Seoul.

1999 January 1st: The 1st Senior Advisory Committee (SAC) was appointed by the Founder. They were W.Y. Chung (410)

L. Seiberlich (1815)

R. Hanke (4137)

A. Ahpo (10187)

V. Martinov (10189)

1999 January 1st: The 2nd generations of the US TAC members were appointed by the founder. They were:

Robert Shipley (4825) – Neh Gong Bu

Ted Mason (112895) – Neh Gong Bu

Frank Bonsignore (15805) – Neh Gong Bu

Frank Schermerhorn (19787) – Weh Gong Bu

Daymon Kenyon (19839) – Weh Gong Bu

Philip Bartolacci (20571) – Weh Gong Bu

Hyuk Woon Kwon (10805) – Shim Gong Bu

Jeff Moonitz (17650) – Shim Gong Bu

Mary Ann Walsh (17926) – Shim Gong Bu

1999 March 19th-21st: Conducted the Euro Clinic and Demonstration for cerebrating the 25th anniversary of the Moo Duk Kwan in Belgium.

1999 May 14th-15th: Conducted clinics for the U.K. Soo Bahk Do Moo Duk Kwan Federation in Manchester, England.

1999 July 29th-31st: The 21st U.S. Nationals, Houston, TX.

1999 October 22nd-24th: Attended the Greek National Championships to celebrate the 30th anniversary of Moo Duk Kwan in Greece and conducted clinics and demonstration in Athens, Greece.

1999 October 29th-31st: Attended the National Championships to celebrate the 25th anniversary of Moo Duk Kwan in Argentina and conducted clinics and demonstration in Mendoza, Argentina.

1999 November 13th-21st: The 17th U.S. Ko Dan Ja Shim Sa in Highfall. NY

August 31, 1999: Promoted to Gu Dan (9th Dan) in the Moo Duk Kwan

2000's (by year)

2000

2000 February 25th –March 3rd: Conducted the 2nd South East Asia Leadership Seminars (SEALS) in Sibu, Sarawak, Malaysia.

2000 March 4th-5th: Assisted the Founder's Ko Dan Ja Clinics at the Central Do Jang in Seoul.

2000 March 17th-19th: Attended and assisted the annual Euro Clinics in Belgium.

2000 March 31st-April 2nd: Attend the symposium for the "Moo Duk Kwan philosophy in Corporate America" in Atlanta, GA.

2000 April 15th: Attend the 25th anniversary celebration for the U.S. Headquarters Do Jang in Springfield, NJ.

2000 May 12th-13th: Assisted the Founder's Ko Dan Ja Clinics at the Central Do Jang in Seoul.

2000 June 9th-17th: The 18th U.S. Ko Dan Ja Shim Sa in Carbondale, CO.

2000 June 23rd-25th: International Summer Camp in Elka Park, NY. The new Soo Bahk Do Ki Cho was introduced.

2000 July 15th-22nd: Conducted the Euro Swiss Summer Camp at the Piz Beverin in Swiss Alps.

2000 August 18th-20th: Conducted the U.K. National Clinics at the Clayton Green Sport Centre in Manchester, England.

2000 August 25th-27th: The U.S. National Summer Camp at Fort Casey, WA.

2000 September 22nd-October 1st: Organized the Millennium Visit with the Founder in Korea.

2000 October 6th-8th: The U.S. National Camp at the Camp Fern in Marshall, TX.

2000 November 8th-12th: The 22nd U.S. Nationals in Mount Vernon, NJ.

2000 November 16th-20th: Conducted clinics for the Mexico Moo Duk Kwan in Mexico City, Aguas Caliente, and Pachuca.

2001

2001 February 23rd-March 1st: Conducted the 3rd South East Asia Leadership Seminars (SEALS) in Miri, Sarawak, Malaysia

2001 March 3rd-4th: Assisted the Founder's Ko Dan Ja Clinics at the Central Do Jang in Seoul.

2001 March 15th-18th: Attended and assisted the annual Euro Clinics in Belgium. The Goodwill championships took placed between team of Euro and U.S.A.

2001 May 15th-16th: Assisted the Founder's Ko Dan Ja Clinics at the Central Do Jang in Seoul.

2001 June 1st-9th: The 19th U.S. Ko Dan Ja Shim Sa, at the Camp Pontiac in NY. The Moment of Master weekend started from this event.

2001 June 24th-30th: Conducted the Euro Camp in Agistri Island in Greece

2001 July 25th-28th: The 23rd U.S. Nationals at the Town & Country Hotel in San Diego, CA.

2001 August 17th-21st: Organized visits with the Founder in Korea and had a demonstration in Yoju City. Futur Korea Ko Dan Ja Shim Sa was discussed with the founder.

2001 October 3rd-4th: Assisted the Founder's Ko Dan Ja Clinics at the Central Do Jang in Korea.

2002

2002 February 11th-12th: Assisted the Founder's Ko Dan Ja clinics at the Central Do Jang in Seoul. The 1st Ko Ko Dan Ja Shim Sa plan was made for the 2002.

2002 February 28th-March 3rd: The U.S. Studio team and Leadership seminars at the Meadowland Sheraton Hotel in Meadowland, NJ.

2002 March 14th-18th: Assisted the annual Euro Clinics in Warve, Belgium.

2002 May 11th-12th: Assisted the Founder's Ko Dan Ja Clinics at the Central Do Jang in Seoul.

2002 May 16th-20th: Conducted clinics at cities of Aguas Caliente, Guadalajara, and Irapuato in Mexico.

2002 June 13th-22nd: The 20th U.S. Ko Dan Ja Shim Sa in Carbondale, CO.

2002 June 26th-July 2nd: Conducted the 4th South East Asia Leadership Seminars (SEALS) in Darwin, Austral

2002 July 14th: **Father / Founder: Hwang Kee passes away.**

2002 July 20th: The World Moo Duk Kwan and the Korean Soo Bahk Do Association called the special Board o Director's meeting for the new successor. Jin Mun Hwang (aka H. C. Hwang) became as the 2nd Kwan Jang Nim for the Moo Duk Kwan.

2002 July 31st-August 3rd: The 24th U.S. Nationals at the Sheraton Hotel in East Rutherford, NJ. This Nationa was contributed to memory of the Founder of the Moo Duk Kwan. The inaugural ceremony of the 2nd Kwan Jang Nim for the Moo Duk Kwan took placed.

2002 September 28th: The inaugural ceremony of the 2nd Kwan Jang Nim for the Moo Duk Kwan took placed at the Central Do Jang in Seoul, Korea.

2002 October 3rd-9th: The week long 1st Korea Ko Dan Ja Shim Sa at Dae Doon Mountain in Korea.

2002 November 1st-3rd: Met with the U.S. Senior Advisory Committee (SAC) to discuss future of the Moo Duk Kwan in Randolph, NJ (Birth of the President Vision Tour).

2002 November 6th-11th: Conducted clinics and shared the Vision in Cordoba, Argentina (The beginning of the PVT)

2002 November: Announces Vision Tour I, world tour to begin in 2003

2002 December 10th-11th, Conducted the Ko Dan Ja Clinics at the Central Do Jang in Korea.

July 2002 - Present: Serving as the President of the World Moo Duk Kwan and the Life President of the U.S. Soo Bahk Do Moo Duk Kwan Federation

2003

2003: The World wide Vision Tour to relate Moo Duk Kwan History and Traditions. To share Objectives for the Moo Duk Kwan in the upcoming years.

His motivation was as follows, "***Our beloved Founder of the Moo Duk Kwan, Grandmaster Hwang Kee passed away on July 14, 2002. Upon his passing, Grandmaster Hwang Kee became part of the Past. We are the present, and the future of the Moo Duk Kwan. It is dependant upon us and our actions. Now is a very important time in the Moo Duk Kwan's history for the present members to "Strengthen the foundation" of the Art so that the foundation will carry and ensure the future longevity of out art into the next generations***"

2003 January 11th: The first Vision Tour at Honesdale, PA

2003 January 25th: The PVT at Houston, TX

2003 February 1st: The PVT at Carlsbad, CA

2003 February 8th: The PVT at Bradley, IL

2003 February 15th: The PVT at Danbury, CT.

2003 February 22nd; The PVT at Atlanta, GA

2003 February 26th: The PVT at the Ko Dan Ja Clinics in Seoul, Korea.

2003 March 13th-17th: The PVT at the annual Euro Clinics in Warve, Belgium.

2003 March 26th-30th: The PVT at the U.S. Leadership seminars in Meadowland, NJ

2003 April 20th: The PVT at Santa Barbara, CA

2003 April 25th: The PVT at Cherry Hill, NJ

2003 May 3rd: The PVT at Myrtle Beach, SC

2003 May 16th-24th, The PVT at the 21st US Ko Dan Ja Shim Sa and the Moment of Master weekend in Bethany Louisiana.

2003 June 19th; The PVT at Manhasset, NY

2003 June 18th-29th: The PVT at the first week long Euro Ko Dan Ja Shim Sa in Agistri island, Greece

2003 July 1st-2nd: The PVT and clinics for the Italian Moo Duk Kwan in Rome, Italy.

2003 July 7th: The PVT at New Windsor, NY

2003 July 8th: The PVT at Fishkill,, NY

2003 July 10th: The PVT at Kingston, NY

2003 July 11th: The PVT at Ellenville, NY

2003 July 12th: The PVT at Binghamton, NY

2003 July 16th: The PVT at Baltimore, MD

2003 July 17th: The PVT at Williamstown, NJ

2003 July 18th: The PVT at Cherry Hill, NJ

2003 July 19th: The PVT at Freehold, NJ

2003 July 26th-30th: The PVT at the 25th U.S. Nationals and the 1st World Moo Duk Kwan Designee's Symposium in Meadowland, NJ

2003 September 4th-8th; The PVT at the United Kingdom National Clinic in Manchester, England.

2003 October 2nd-9th: The PVT at the 2nd Korea Ko Dan Ja Shim Sa in Dan Yang, Chun Ra Province.

2003 October 23rd: The PVT at St. Cloud, MN

2003 October 24th: The PVT at St. Paul, MN

2003 October 31st: The PVT at New Milford, CT.

2003 November 7th: The PVT at Ft. Lauderdale, FL.

2003 November 8th: The PVT at Mobile, AL.

2003 November 9th: The PVT at Atlanta, GA

2003 December 12th: The PVT at Bradley, IL.

2003 December 13th: The PVT at Lakewood, OH.

2003 December 14th: The PVT at Marquette, MI.

2003 December 15th: The PVT at Southgate, MI.

2004

2004 January 11th: The PVT at Chesapeake, VA

2004 January 23rd-31st: The PVT at the 22nd U.S. Ko Dan Ja Shim Sa and the Moment with Master weekend in Mobile, AL.

2004 February 21st: The PVT at Springfield, NJ

2004 February 27th: The PVT at Seoul, Korea.

2004 March 17th: The PVT at Camas, WA

2004 March 18th: Channel Town, WA

2004 March 19th, The PVT at Wenatchee, WA

2004 March 25th-27th: The PVT at the annual Euro Clinics in Warve, Belgium.

2004 April 13th: The PVT at Santa Barbara, CA.

2004 April 14th: The PVT at Torrance, CA.

2004 April 15th: The PVT at Aliso Viejo, CA.

2004 April 16th: The PVT at San Diego, CA.

2004 April 17th: The PVT at Carlsbad, CA.

2004 April 21st: The PVT at Tulsa, OK.

2004 April 22nd: The PVT at Dallas, TX.

2004 April 23rd: The PVT at Carthage, TX.

2004 April 24th: The PVT at Houston, TX.

2004 May 2nd: The PVT at Myrtle Beach, SC.

2004 May 21st: The PVT at Danbury, CT.

2004 June 2nd-8th: The PVT at the 5th SEALS (South East Asia Leadership Seminars) in Bintulu, Sarawak, Malaysia (The official Australian National Federation was formed and recognized during the event)

2004 June 12th-13th: The PVT at Clinics at the Central Do Jang in Seoul.

2004 June 19th: The PVT at Manhasset, NY.

2004 June 26th: The PVT at Red Stone, CO.

2004 July 10th-17th: The PVT at the Euro Swiss Camp at Piz Beverin in Swiss Alps.

2004 August 18th-21st: The PVT at the 26th U.S. Nationals at the Town & Country Hotel in San Diego, CA.

2004 September 24th-27th: The PVT at the U.K. National clinics in Manchester, England.

2004 October 7th-15th: The PVT at the 3rd Korea Ko Dan Ja Shim Sa in Tcheong Pyung, Korea

2004 October 23rd: The PVT at Cherry Hill, NJ.

2004 October 30th: The PVT at Middleton, MA.

2004 November 1st-6th: The PVT at the 1st week long Ko Dan Ja Shim Sa for the South American Region which was held in Mendoza, Argentina.

2004 November 11th-17th: The PVT at the 2nd World Moo Duk Kwan Designee Symposium at Guadalajara, Mexico.

2004 December 14th: The PVT at Springfield, NJ.

2004: "Man of the Year" for Black Belt Magazine

2005

2005 January 7th-14th: The PVT at the 23rd U.S. Ko Dan Ja Shim Sa and the Moment with Master weekend in Ramona, CA.

2005 March 12th-13th: The PVT at the Instructor's clinics at the Central Do Jang in Korea.

2005 March 19th-25th: The PVT at the 2nd Euro Ko Dan Ja Shim Sa in Belgium.

2005 March 25th-26th: The PVT at the Annual Euro Clinics in Warve, Belgium.

2005 April 23rd: The PVT at the Instructor's clinics at the Headquarters Do Jang in Springfield, NJ.

2005 April 29th: The PVT at Myrtle Beach, SC.

2005 May 7th: The PVT at Hudson Valley Region in NY

2005 May 21st: The PVT at Detroit, MI

2005 May 27th: The PVT at Liberty, NY

2005 June 11th: The PVT at the Headquarters Do Jang in Springfield, NJ

2005 June 25th: The PVT at Springfield, NJ.

2005 July 4th-15th: The 3rd anniversary for the Founder's passing memorial in Korea

2005 July 21st-23rd: The PVT at the 27th U.S. Nationals at the Double Tree Hotel in Orlando, FL.

2005 July 22nd: Appointed the 3rd Generation of U.S. TAC members. They were;

Steve Diaz (19461) – Neh Gong Bu

Frank Schermerhorn (19787) – Neh Gong Bu

Cash Cooper (23082) – Neh Gong Bu

Daymon Kenyon (19839) – Weh Gong Bu

Craig Hays (23132) – Weh Gong Bu

Jeff Griggs (23269) – Weh Gong Bu

Philip Bartolacci (20571) – Shim Gong Bu –Chairperson

Dae Kyu Jang (20780) – Shim Gong Bu

Ken Trevelyan (21909) – Shim Gong Bu

2005 July 23: Forms the Hu Kyu In: Objective is to maintain, preserve, and perpetuate he History and Traditions Soo Bahk Do Moo Duk Kwan, sharing it's knowledge, experience with its members and their community.

Members include:

A. Robert Shipley, (#4825)

B. Hyuk Yoon Kwon, (#10805)

C. Ted Mason, (#12895)

D. Frank Bonsignore, (#15805)

F. Arthur Pryor, (#16505) 2005-2009

H. Jeffery Moonitz, (#17650)

I. Mary Ann Walsh, (#17926) Deceased: August 22nd , 2012

J. Wilton Bennett, (#19027)

Fred Messersmith, (#20729)

** 2009 Frank Schermerhorn,(#19787) added as liaison to T.A.C. (Technical, Advisory, Committee)

** 2012 Phillip Bartolacci, (20571) added

2005 July 29th: The 2004 Black Belt Men of the Year Award ceremony and banquet at the Global theatre Universal Studio in Hollywood, CA

2005 July 30th: The PVT at Hollywood, CA and later at the Santa Barbara, CA.

2005 July 31st: The PVT at Torrance, CA.

2005 August 1st: The PVT at Carlsbad. CA

2005 August 27th: The PVT at Yakoma, WA

2005 September 10th: The PVT at Minneapolis, MN

2005 September 23rd-29th: The PVT at the 4th Korea Ko Dan Ja Shim Sa in Sok Tcho, Kang Won Province.

2005 September 28th-30th: The PVT at the 3rd World Moo Duk Kwan Designee Symposium at Sok Tcho.

2005 September 30th-October 2nd: The 60th years of Moo Duk Kwan anniversary celebration in Sok Tcho, Kar Won Province, Korea.

2005 October 6th: The PVT at Tcheong Ju, Korea.

2005 October 23rd: The PVT at Myrtle Beach, SC.

2005 October 28th-29th: The PVT at Silver Spring, MD

2005 November 5th: The PVT at Freehold, NJ.

2005 November 7th-14th: The PVT at the South American clinic at Santiago and Vina Del Mar in Chile.

2005 November 11: The PVT at Vina Del Mar in Chile.

2005 November 19th: The PVT at the Instructor's class in Springfield, NJ.

2005: December 16th-17th: The PVT at the member's clinics at the Central Do Jang in Seoul.

2006

2006 January 13th-15th: The PVT at the U.S. Moment of Master weekend at Mobile, AL

2006 January 13th–20th: The PVT at the 24th U.S. Ko Dan Ja Shim Sa with new TAC in Mobile, AL.

2006 February 11th: The PVT at the Instructor's clinic for the U.S. Region 2 in Springfield, NJ.

2006 March 11th: The PVT at Stratford, CT.

2006 March 17th-18th: The Hu Kyun In's weekend (The first Guardians of the Art Seminars) at the Headquarters Do Jang in Springfield, NJ.

2006 March 24th-26th: The PVT at the Annual Euro Clinics in Warve, Belgium.

2006 April 22nd: The PVT at the U.S. Region 2 Dan Shim Sa at the Piscataway High School in NJ.

2006 April 28th-29th: The PVT at Myrtle Beach, SC.

2006 May 21st: The PVT at the Instructor's clinics at the Central Do Jang in Seoul.

2006 May 26th-28th: The PVT at cities of Lagos de Moreno, Jalisco, and Mexico City.

2006 June 3rd: The PVT at the Instructor's clinic at the Hqs School in Springfield, NJ.

2006 June 24th: The PVT at Williamstown, NJ.

2006 July 15th-22nd: The PVT at the Euro Swiss Camp in Switzerland.

2006 July 28th-30th: Conducted the PVT related seminars at the Black Belt sponsored seminars in Long Beach, CA.

2006 August 10th-12th: The PVT at the 28th U.S. Nationals, San Diego, CA. Jin Tae Hwang (11) was a special guest for the U.S, Nationals,

2006 August 14th: The PVT at Santa Barbara, CA.

2006 September 8th: Visited with Master Walter Okahara (31147) to present his 4th Dan certificates and belt. He passed on September 11, 2006.

2006 September 15th: U.S.A. Leadership Objectives introduced:

A. Strengthen our foundation

B. Emphasize the Moo Duk Kwan's uniqueness

C. Covey our History

D. Strengthen our five Moo Do Values

E. Increase education

F. Increase public visibility

G. Financial stability

2006 September 16th: The PVT at the Ko Dan Ja Class in Springfield, NJ.

2006: September 21st-28th: The PVT at the 5th Korea Ko Dan Ja Shim Sa at the Dawit Mountain in Korea.

2006: October 17th-20th: The PVT at the 4th World Moo Duk Kwan Designee Symposium in Crete, Greece.

2006 October 21st-22nd: Conduct the International Clinics and Demonstration in Crete, Greece.

2006 October 21st-28th: The PVT at the 3rd Euro Ko Dan Ja Shim Sa in Create, Greece

2006 November 9th-13th: The PVT at the South America Region Clinics in Montevideo, Uruguay.

2006 November 18th: The PVT at the Instructors clinics in Springfield, NJ.

2006: December 2nd: The PVT at the Instructors clinics in Gillett, NJ.

2007

2007 January 25th-26th: The PVT at the U.S. Moment with Master weekend in Ramona, CA.

2007 January 26th–February 2nd: The PVT at the 25th U.S. Ko Dan Ja Shim Sa in Ramona, CA. Special sessions for Hwa Sun Hyung for SAC (Senior Advisory Committee member) and Chil Dan candidates.

2007 February 22nd: The PVT at the Instructors clinics in Dae Ku, Korea

2007 February 24th: Conducted Hwa Sun Hyung clinic for SAC members in Korea.

2007 February 26th: Conducted a special clinic for foreign visitors from Australia and Belgium at the Central D Jang in Seoul.

2007 February 28th: The PVT at the Instructor's clinics at the Central Do Jang in Seoul.

2007 March 23rd-25th: The PVT at the Annual Euro Clinics in Andenne, Belgium.

2007 April 20th-24th: The PVT at the 6th SEALS (South East Asia Leadership Seminars) in Canberra, Australia. The international Youth Leadership Program was discussed for the first time.

2007 April 28th: Attended the Board of Director's meeting for the Korean Soo Bahk Do Association.

2007 May 2nd: The PVT at the Instructor's clinics at the Central Do Jang in Seoul.

2007 June 3rd: The PVT at the U.S. Region 3 in Myrtle Beach, SC.

2007 June 16th: Conducted the Hwa Sun Hyung clinic for U.S. Hu Kyun In members in Middletown, NY.

2007 July 8th: Conducted the National PVT Tele-Conference.

2007 July 28th: The PVT at the 30th years of anniversary at the Winding River Do Jang in Binghamton, NY.

2007 August 22nd-26th: The PVT at the 29th U.S. National Festival at the Town & Country Hotel in San Diego, CA. It was the first year to adopt the new format with the Moo Do festival. HC Hwang KJN demonstrated the Hwa Sun Hyung.

2007 September 28th-October 4th: The PVT at the 6th Korea Ko Dan Ja Shim Sa in Pal Kong San, Dae Ku, Korea

2007 October 7th: Conducted the National Soo Bahk Do Demonstration at Dae Ku, Korea.

2007 October 8th: The PVT at the Instructor's class at the Central Do Jang in Yong San, Seoul.

2007 October 26th-27th: The PVT at the U.S. Region 9 Dan Shim Sa in Santa Barbara, CA.

2007 November 9th-15th: The PVT at the 2nd South America Ko Dan Ja Shim Sa in Mendoza, Argentina.

2007: November 15th-18th: The PVT at the 5th World Moo Duk Kwan Designee Symposium in Mendoza, Argentina.

2007 November 17th-18th: Attend the International Goodwill Championships for the 33rd years of anniversary of the Moo Duk Kwan in Argentina.

2008

2008 February 23rd-24th: The PVT at the Instructor's clinics at the Neo Gu Ri Village in An Seong, Kyong Ki Province where was the 2008 Korea Ko Dan Ja site.

2008 March 13th-16th: The PVT at the Annual Euro Clinics in Bruxelle, Belgium. Hwa Sun Hyung classes for Senior Dans in Euro.

2008 March 29th: The PVT at the Hwa Sun Hyung Clinics for 6th Dan and higher ranks for the East coast region in Springfield, NJ.

2008 April 18th-19th: The PVT at the U.S. Region 5 Dan Shim Sa in Cleveland, OH.

2008 May 3rd: The PVT at the U.S. Region 2 Dan Shim Sa in Piscataway, NJ.

2008 May 10th: The PVT at the 121st Dan Shim Sa at the Central Do Jang in Yong San, Seoul.

2008 May 23rd-25th: The PVT at the clinics at Mexico City and Agua Caliente, Mexico

2008 June 21st-22nd: The PVT at the 1st South Jersey Moo Duk Kwan Festival in Pennsville, NJ

2008 June 28th: The PVT at the Instructor's Hyung clinics in Springfield, NJ

2008: July 5th-11th: The PVT at the 4th Euro Ko Dan Ja Shim Sa in Wald, Switzerland.

2008 July 12th-19th: The PVT at the Euro Swiss Summer Camp in Thusis, Switzerland.

2008 August 14th-16th: The PVT at the 30th U.S. National Festival at the Town & Country Hotel in San Diego, CA.

2008 August 15th-22nd: The PVT at the U.S. 26th Ko Dan Ja Shim Sa at Town & Country Hotel in San Diego and moved to Ramona on August 17th and finished the Shim Sa in Ramona, CA.

2008: October 17th-23rd, The PVT at the 7th Korea Ko Dan Ja Shim Sa at Neo Gu Ri Village in An Seong, Korea.

2008 November 14th-17th: The PVT at the Greek National Clinics and Championships in Glyfada, Athens, Greece

2008 November 18th-23rd: The PVT at the 6th World Moo Duk Kwan Designee's Symposium at Spa, Belgium.

2008 December 13th-17th: The PVT at the 7th SEALS (South East Asia Leadership Seminar) in Limbang, Sarawak, Malaysia.

2008 December 21st: The PVT at the Instructor's Ho Sin Sool Clinic in Dae Ku, Korea

2009

2009 January 31st: Conducted a clinic for the 7th Dan and higher rank at Gillett, NJ

2009 February 7th: The PVT at the Ko Dan Ja / Instructor's clinic in New Windsor, NY.

2009 February 21st: The PVT at the Regional clinic for R1 at Danbury, CT.

2009 March 7th: The PVT at the Ko Dan Ja Hyung clinics at Springfield, NJ.

2009 March 13th-14th: The PVT at the Il Soo Sik clinics at Santa Barbara, CA.

2009 April 17th: Visited Region 5 for Nai Han Ji Hyung clinic with attended Ko Dan Ja.

2009 April 18th: The PVT at the US Region 2 Dan Shim Sa in Pennsville, NJ

2009 May 1st-2nd: The PVT at the US Region 3 Dan Shim Sa in Myrtle Beach, SC.

2009 May 9th-10th: The PVT at the Ko Dan Ja / Instructor's clinics at the Central Do Jang in Seoul.

2009 June 20th: The PVT at the 2nd South Jersey Moo Duk Kwan Festival at Pennsville, NJ.

2009 August 27th-29th: The PVT at the 31st U.S. Nationals / Moo Do Festival at the Town & Country Hotel in San Diego, CA. Introduced the new World Moo Duk Kwan patch as well as the Moo Do Chul Hak in English version at the event.

2009 August 29th-September 4th: The PVT at the 27th U.S. Ko Dan Ja Shim Sa, at Ramona, CA.

2009 September 12th: Photo taking session for Hwa Sun Hyung, Chil Song Hyungs, and Yuk Ro Hyungs in Springfield, NJ.

2009 September 22nd-27th: The PVT at the 7th World Moo Duk Kwan Designee's Symposium in Atlanta, GA. International Youth Leader team attended.

2009 October 11th: The PVT at the 1st Youth Hwa Rang training sessions sponsored by the Moo Duk Kwan Academy, Ellenville, NY

2009 October 17th: The PVT during the TAC tour event at the Region 2 Dan Shim Sa in Binghamton, NY.

2009 October 30th: Conducted and presented demonstration with the 2009 Korea Ko Dan Ja candidates at the Yong Oh Rhum Traditional Martial arts Festival in Yong In, Korea.

2009 October 31st-November 6,th The PVT at the 8th Korea Ko Dan Ja Shim Sa in An Seong, Korea

2009 November 15th-21st: The PVT at the 3rd South America Ko Dan Ja Shim Sa in Mar Del Plata, Argentina.

2009 November 21st: International Clinic and Championships for the 35th years of anniversary of Moo Duk Kwa in Argentina.

2010

2010 January 16th: The PVT at the Williamstown, NJ

2010 January 29th-31st: The PVT at the U.S. TAC training and meeting in Atlanta, GA. Sam Soo Sik was organized and the "Moo Do Ja Seh" was set as the theme for the year.

2010 February 13th: The PVT at the U.S. Region 2 Instructor's clinic at the headquarters Dojang in Springfield, NJ. Sam Soo Sik was introduced.

2010 February 18th-20th: Attended the U.S. SAC (Senior Advisory Committee) training and meeting at Santa Inez, CA. W.Y. Chung (410), H.C. Hwang (509), L. Seiberlich (1815), Russ Hanke (4137), V. Martinov (10189) were attended.

2010 March 1st: Conducted Moo Duk Kwan ambassador Tele-Conference.

2010 March 13th-19th: The PVT at the 5th Euro Ko Dan Ja Shim Sa in Warve, Belgium

2010 March 20st-21nd: The PVT at the Annual Euro Clinics in Warve, Belgium.

2010 March 28th: Attended the Regional Championships in Fishkill, NY.

2010 April 9th-11th: The PVT at the R7 TAC tour (Daymon Kenyon, 19839) in St. Paul, MN

2010 April 17th: The PVT at the R2 Dan Shim Sa in NJ.

2010 April 30th-May 2nd: The PVT at the R3 TAC tour (Ken Trevelyan, 21909) in Inwood, WV.

2010 May 4th: HC Hwang KJN started the Tuesday and Thursday classes at the Headquarters Do Jang in Springfield, NJ.

2010 May 21st-23rd: The PVT at the R2 TAC tour (Dae Kyu Jang, 20780) in Fishkill, NY.

2010 June 17th: The PVT at the Instructor's clinic at the Central Do Jang in Yong San, Seoul.

2010 June 22nd-27th: The PVT at the 8th SEALS (South East Asia Leadership Seminar) in Darwin, Australia.

2010 June 23rd-26th: The PVT at the 8th World Moo Duk Kwan Designee's Symposium, at Darwin, Australia. It was the first Zone representative's symposium.

2010 July 8th-11th: The PVT at the 32nd U.S. Nationals / Moo Do Festival in Cherry Hill, NJ.

2010 July 22nd-25th: The PVT at the Region 10 TAC tour (Daymon Kenyon, 19839) in Ellenberg, WA.

2010 August 7th-14th: The PVT at the Euro Swiss Camp in Switzerland

2010 August 27th-29th: The PVT at the Region 1 TAC tour (Ken Trevelyan, 21909) in Boston, MA.

2010 September 17th-19th: The PVT at the Region 4 TAC tour (Philip Bartolacci, 20571) in Alpharetta, GA.

2010 September 24th-26th: The PVT at the Region 6 TAC tour (Kris Poole, 20632) at Carthage, TX.

2010 October 9th: The PVT at the R2 Dan Shim Sa in Williamstown, NJ

2010 October 15th: Attended and presented demonstration with Ko Dan Ja candidates at the Traditional Martial arts festival at the Khum Jeong Gym in Pusan.

2010 October 16th: The PVT at the special training session and banquet for the 65th Moo Duk Kwan anniversary in Kyong Ju, Korea.

October 16-22, 2010: The PVT at the 9th Korea Ko Dan Ja Shim Sa, in Kyong Ju, Korea

November 12-14, 2010: The PVT at the U.S. Moment with Master weekend in Ramona, CA.

2010 November 12th-19th: The PVT at the 28th U.S. Ko Dan Ja Shim Sa, in Ramona, CA.

2011

2011 January 19th: Attended the Tele-Conference for the Moo Duk Kwan Ambassador sponsored by Terri Coffee (28912)

2011 January 25th: Korean Soo Bahk Do members visited the Headquarters for training.

2011 February 26th: The PVT at the Williamstown, NJ. Theme was the Moo Do Ja Seh.

2011 March 18th-19th: The PVT at the TAC tour (Craig Hays, 23132) for the U.S. Region 2 at the Headquarters Do Jang in Springfield, NJ

2011 March 25th-27th: Attended and assisted the Annual Euro Clinic and General Meeting in Warve, Belgium.

2011 April 14th-16th: The PVT at the TAC tour (Daymon Kenyon, 19839) and Region 9 Dan Shim Sa at Torrance, CA. The concept of "START" program was started with assistance of V. Martinov (10189), D. Kenyo (19839), J. Mahony (28537), and J. Duncan (29793).

2011 April 30th-May 1st: The PVT at the U.S. Region 3 Dan Shim Sa & Instructor's clinics in Myrtle Beach, S

2011 May 4th: Conducted the U.S. SAC (Senior Advisory Committee) Tele-Conference for the "START (Share The ART)" program.

2011 May 14th: Conducted the 127th Dan Shim Sa and PVT at the Central Do Jang in Yong San, Seoul.

2011 May 15th: The PVT at the Instructor's clinic at the Central Do Jang in Yong San, Seoul.

2011 June 1st: The 4th Generation of the U.S. TAC was appointed. They were:

Cash Cooper (23082 - Chairman

Bill Nelson (21420) – Neh Gong Bu

Lisa Kozak (23540) – Neh Gong Bu

Josh Lockwood (29577) – Neh Gong Bu

Daymon Kenyon (19839) – Weh Gong Bu

Craig Hays (23132) – Weh Gong Bu

Jeff Griggs (23269) – Weh Gong Bu

Kris Poole (20632) – Shim Gong Bu

Dae Kyu Jang (20780) – Shim Gong Bu

Jennifer Gibbons (32238) – Shim Gong Bu

2011 June 1st: Conducted Tele-Conference for promoting the "START" program. The U.S. HKI (Hu Kyun In), TAC (Technical Advisory Committee). BOD (Board of Directors), and NPVT (National PVT Committee) were attended the conference.

2011 June 18th: The PVT at the U.S. Region 2 Hwa Rang Camp.

2011 June 10th: The PVT at the Manhasset, NY

2011 June 26th – July 2nd: The PVT at the Euro Summer Camp in Marathon, Greece.

2011 July 6th-9th: The 33rd U.S. Nationals / Moo Do Festival at the Town & Country Hotel in San Diego, CA.

2011 July 21st-24th: The PVT at the U.S. Region 10 TAC tour (C. Cooper, 23082, J. Gibbons, 32238) and Summer Camp.

2011 October 15th-21st: The PVT at the 10th Korea Ko Dan Ja Shim Sa in An Seong, Korea.

2011 November 4th-10th: The PVT at the 4th South America Ko Dan Ja Shim Sa in Mendoza, Argentina.

2011 November 7th-11th: The PVT at the 9th World Moo Duk Kwan Designee's Symposium in Mendoza, Argentina

2011 November 11th-18th: The PVT at the 29th U.S. Ko Dan Ja Shim Sa, in Ramona, CA.

2011 December 2nd-6th: The PVT at the 9th SEALS (South East Asia Leadership Seminar) in Miri, Sarawak, Malaysia

2011 December 10th-11th: The PVT at the Instructor's clinic in Ja Yu Dae Ryun in Tchoong Ju, Korea.

2012

2012 February 25th: The PVT at the Instructor's class in Springfield, NJ.

2012 March 30th: The PVT at the Annual Euro Clinics and Championships in Athens, Greece

2012 April 1st-7th: The PVT at the 6th Euro Ko Dan Ja Shim Sa in Glyfada, Athens, Greece.

2012 April 13th-15th: Attended and assisted the Region 5 Dan Shim Sa and clinics at Merrillville, IN.

2012 April 19th: The PVT at Santa Barbara, CA

2012 April 20th-21st: Attended and assisted the Region 9 Dan Shim Sa and clinics in Santa Barbara, CA.

2012 May 1st: The PVT at Williamstown, NJ.

2012 May 3rd-5th: The PVT at the Region 3 Dan Shim Sa and clinics in Myrtle Beach, SC

2012: May 13th: The PVT at the 129th Classing Dan Shim Sa and Clinic at the Central Do Jang in Yong San, Seoul, Korea.

2012 June 8th-9th: The PVT at the Manhasset, NY.

June 27-30, 2012: The 34th U.S. National Festival in Cherry Hill, NJ. USA

2012 July 12th: Visited and trained with young generation of Ko Dan Ja at the Headquarters Do Jang in Springfield, NJ

2012 July 29th- August 4th: The PVT at the Euro Swiss Summer Camp at the Piz Beverin, in Swiss Alps.

2012 September 29th: Attended the Binghamton, NY for the 40th years of Moo Duk Kwan of Frank Schermerhorn (19787)

2012 October 12th-18th: The PVT at the 11th Korea Ko Dan Ja Shim Sa at Pal Gong Mountain, Dae Ku, Korea.

2012 October 20th: The PVT at the 130th Dan Shim Sa and clinics at the Central Do Jang in Yong San.

2012 November 9th-11th: The PVT at the Moment with Master weekend in Ramona, CA.

2012 November 11th-15th: The 10th World Moo Duk Kwan Designees (Zone) Symposium in Ramona, CA.USA

2012 November 9th-16th: The 30th U.S. Ko Dan Ja Shim Sa in Ramona, CA.

2012 December 8th: Guardians of the Art #2 seminar, Springfield, NJ.

2013

2013 October 2nd: S.E.A.L.S. (South / East / Asian/ Leadership / Seminars) Adelaide, Australia

2013 October 29th: Conducted,11th World Moo Duk Kwan Symposium, Athens, Greece
Objectives: A. Youth Leadership
B. Standardization of Jo-Kyo / Kyo-Sa / Sa Bom certification
C. Preparation for 70th Celebration, Seoul, Korea in 2015

2013 March 1st: 7th Euro Ko Dan Ja Shim Sa, Belgium

2013 March 22nd: Euro Seminars, Belgium.

2013 May: Euro Soo Bahk Do seminars Athens, Greece

2013 July 17th: 35th U.S. National Festival, Cherry Hill NJ.

2013 July 27th: Conducted,7th Euro Ko Dan Ja Shim Sa, Wald, Switzerland

2013 September 14th: Conducted, Ko Dan Ja Shim Sa, Moo Do Festival, and seminars, Cordoba, Argentina

2013 October 11th: Conducted,12th Ko Dan Ja Shim Sa, Seoul, Korea

2013 November 15th: Conducted,30th Ko Dan Ja Shim Sa, San Diego, CA.

2014

2014 January: Vision Tour II tour Announced

2014 March: 21st-30th, Conducted, Euro Ko Dan Ja Shim Sa

2014 April 11th-13th, Attended PVT 2, Region 5, U.S.A. and Dan Shim Sa

2014 July 17th-21st: 36th U.S. National Festival, Salt Lake City, UT.

2014 July 25th-Aug.4th: Euro Summer Camp, Switzerland

2014 October 17th-26th: 13th Ko Dan Ja Shim Sa, Seoul, Korea

2014 November 6th-9th: World Moo Duk Kwan symposium, Puerto Rico

2014 November 14th-21st: 31st Ko Dan Ja Shim Sa, USA, San Diego, CA.

2015

70th Anniversary of the Moo Duk Kwan

2015 January 17th: USA Region 2 Alpha team seminar at the HQ Dojang in Springfield, NJ

2015 February 9-11th: The trial (IP Protection) in Scranton Federal court, PA

2015 February 13-15th: PVT II tour in Region 4, USA

2015 February 27 – March 1st: East Coast Winter Camp in Connecticut

2015 March 7th: 7th Dan and Up training session at the HQ Dojang in Springfield, NJ

2015 March 21-27th: The 8th Euro Ko Dan Ja Shim Sa in Belgium

2015 March 27-29th: Annual Euro Seminars in Belgium

2015 April 18th: The 135th Dan Shim Sa in Region 2, USA

2015 April 21-28th: The 135th Dan Shim Sa at the Central HQ in Seoul / Preparing the Moo Duk Kwan 70th celebration in Korea.

2015 June 6th: USA Region 1 tournament for the US SBD MDK Foundation

2015 July 23rd – 26th: attended Region 10 Summer Camp

2015 July 30th – August 2nd: attended 37th U.S. National Festival, Garden Grove, Ca. (I believe it was Boston areas of MA)

2015 August 17th: Wining from the trial for the protection of the name Moo Duk Kwan

2015 October 23rd – 29th: Conducted 14th Korean Ko Dan Ja Shim Sa, Kang Hwa Kun, In Cheon, South Korea

2015 October 26th – 29th: attended World Moo Duk Kwan symposium, Kang Hwa Kun, In Cheon, South Korea

2015 October 30th – November 1st: attended World Moo Duk Kwan 70th anniversary celebration in Suwon, South Korea

2015 November 13th – 20th: Conducted 32nd U.S. Ko Dan Ja Shim Sa, Ramona, Ca.

2016

2016 February 17th: 7th Dan and up training session at the HQ Dojang in Springfield, NJ

2016 March 12th, Attended Region 10 championship tournament.

2016 March 18th-20th, Attended Region 1 tournament, Boston, Ma

2016 March 25th – 27th, Attended Euro meeting and seminars, Zurich, Switzerland

2016 April 16th: Attended Region 2 Dan Shim Sa

2016 April 25th _ May 2nd: Conducted 137th Dan Shim Sa, and clinics, Seoul, Korea

2016 May 13th-15th: Attended Region 3 Dan Shim Sa, Myrtle Beach, SC.

2016 June 29th – July3rd: Attended the 38th U.S. National Festival, Anaheim, Ca.

2016 July 29th – August 6th: Attended Euro Summer Camp, Switzerland

2016 August 19-21st: US East Coast Spirit Weekend training at the HQ Do Jang in Springfield, NJ

2016 September 22nd – 26th: Conducted seminars, Melbourne, Australia

2016 October 7th – 13th: Attended the 1st World Moo Duk Kwan youth Leadership Symposium, Kang Hwa Ku In Cheon, South Korea

2016 October 7th – 14th: Conducted 15th Korean Ko Dan Ja Shim Sa, Kyei Myung Won, Kang Hwa Kun, In Cheon, South Korea

2016 October 15th: Conducted Korean 138th Dan Shim Sa, Seoul, Korea

2016 October 16th: Tae Kwon Do (Moo Duk Kwan heritage) practitioners were invited to the Central HQ Do Ja for Seminars for the Moo Do identity.

2016 October 21st – 27th: conducted South American Ko Dan Ja Shim Sa, Uruguay

2016 October 26th– 29th: attended 11th World Moo Duk Kwan zone symposium, Uruguay

2016 October 28-29th: South America Moo Do Festival in Uruguay

2016 November 4-6th: The 10th Years of Moo Duk Kwan in Spain and the 6th Moo Do Festival in Palma Del Malloca.

2016 November 11th – 18th: Conducted 33rd U.S. Ko Dan Ja Shim Sa, Ramona, Ca.

2016 November 11th – 13th: Attended the USA Moment with the Masters, Ramona, Ca.

2016 December 3rd: USA Region 1 & 2 Spirit Weekend training.

2017

2017 January 27th – 29th: Attended Region I Winter Camp

2017 February 11th: 7th Dan and up training in Region 2 at the MDK HQ

2017 March 4th: Attended the 70th year Birthday clinic and cerebration. Clinics held at the MDK HQ and celebration was held at the Iberia restraint in Newark, NJ

2017 March 18th – 24th: Attended the 9th Euro Ko Dan Ja Shim Sa which was held in Athens, Greece.

2017 April 14th – 16th: Attended the 139th Dan Shim Sa and Instructor's clinic at the Central HQ in Seoul, Korea.

2017 April 29th: Attended the 139th Region 2 USA Dan Shim Sa.

2017 May 5th – 7th: Attended the 139th Region 3 USA Dan Shim Sa in Myrtle Beach, S.C.

2017 June 3rd: Attended tournament held by Region 1 USA in Connecticut.

2017 June 10th: Attended a Dan certificates presentation ceremony at the Kwon's SBD Dojang in Manhasset, NY

2017 June 23rd: Attended Gup Shim Sa at the Hwang SBD in Gillette, NJ

2017 July 28th – 30th: Attended Region 10 USA summer camp in Washington State.

2017 August 10th- 12th Attended the 39th U.S. National Festival, Montgomery ,TX.
2017: August 10th: <u>Introduced the New 5th generation of T.A.C. members for the USA</u>: This was made to help increase the visible action of the art to the world though various forms of media and further the growth of the art, and also to support studio owners and the membership. This is also the first time that TAC assistants were added to help serve the TAC and the membership.

The following were selected as the new technical adversary committee members:

Technical (Ki Sul Bu) – Jeff Griggs SBN 23269 / Jen Gibbons SBN 32238
- Define technical standards & improve quality of Shim Gung/Neh Gung/Weh Gung
- Define TAC event clinic material, structure, and perform instruction
- Nationals competition oversight and supervision
- Performance of technical content for SBD institute distribution
- TAC tour content definition
- Coordinate with Digital Media, Administration, and MDK Preservation to align content and standards with work products deployed to the organization

Digital Media (Digital Bu) – Thomas Thai SBN 32244 / Frank Tsai SBN 32700
- SBD institute administration and content definition
- Event filming & content distribution
- MDK advertisement and awareness programs through social media (twitter, Facebook, YouTube, etc)
- Historical preservation of MDK through social media, SBD institute, and documentation
- Education of membership at events through social media (communication of history)
- Coordinate with MDK Preservation to further the goals of spreading the art and awareness of MDK

MDK Preservation (Jin Heung Bu) – Cort Stinehour SBN 33190 / Jared Rosenthal SBN 32740
- Define studio & teaching programs to support membership growth
- Define studio business operations programs to support studio growth
- Perform regular touch points/calls/interfaces with REX and studio owners
- Define studio retention programs
- Coordinate with Digital Media & Administration Bu to facilitate content distribution and tools for the studios

Administration (Heng Jeung Bu) – Josh Lockwood SBN 29755 / Michael Zickafoose SBN 30699
- Define administration process improvements to simplify studio owner burden (Dan testing processes, paperwork, etc.)
- Support National event administration, documentation, & process support (Nationals divisions, KDJ manual updates, process, etc.)
- TAC instructional content documentation for regional distribution
- Coordinate with MDK Preservation, Ki Sul, and Digital Media Bu to facilitate delivery of work products to be deployed to the organization

TAC Chairman – Craig Hays 23132
- Supervise and direct the TAC
- Deliver instruction and event organization
- Serve at the discretion of the President of Moo Duk Kwan
- Coordinate with SAC, HKI, BOD to ensure preservation of the Federation's charter
- Serve as US representative to the World Moo Duk Kwan

TAC Assistants (The first time in history TAC Assistants were added)
- Rodrigo Cruz SBN 33484 (Technical & Digital Media)
- Brian Corrales SBN 36364 (Technical & Digital Media)
- Josh Duncan SBN 29793 (Technical)
- Sue Fittanto SBN 41586 (Digital Media & Preservation)
- Master Ed Horni 36429 (Administration)

2017 August 21st – 27th Attended the 1st Euro Summer Camp, Palma De Mallorca, Islas Baleares, Spain

2017 September 9th: Attended the final ceremony for late Robert M. Shipley IV Sa Bom Nim' passing in Hawaii

2017 October 14th: Attended the 140th Dan Shim Sa at the Region 2 USA.

2017 October 20th – 26th: Conducted the Korean 16th Ko Dan Ja Shim Sa, Seoul, Korea

2017 October 20th -26th: Attended the 2nd World Moo Duk Kwan youth leadership symposium Gang Hwa Do, Korea

2017 October 27th: Conducted seminars for Dan and Youth Leaders in Dae Ku, Korea

2017 November 3rd -5th: Attended the 50th anniversary of the Malaysia Moo Duk Kwan, Miri Malaysia

2017 November 10th – 12th : Attended the Moment with the Masters, Montgomery TX.

2017 November 10th – 17th: Conducted the 34th USA Ko Dan Ja Shim Sa, Montgomery, TX.

2017 November 29th- December 2nd: Attended the World Moo Duk Kwan symposium, Greece
Attending to represent each country:
Jim Class (Puerto Rico, Designee)
Diego Salinas (Spain, Designee)
Kostas Papadopoulos (Greece, Designee) In support: **Stathis Ntaflos (Greece), and Angelo Piskalis Kyo Sa.**
Urs Spoerri (Switzerland, Designee)
Gianni Anile (Italy, Designee) In support: _**Antonello Anile (Italy)**
Kriton Glenn (Australia, Designee)
Mo Vatan (Iran, Designee)
Roberto Fontora Ortiz (Uruguay, Designee)
Alex Carillo Sanhueza (Chile, Designee) In support: **Jacqueline Maturana Olivares (Chile)**
Xavier Dufour (Belgium, Designee) In support: **Laurent Serruys (Belgium).**
Elodie Mollet (France, Designee)
Fabiano Mello (Brazil, Designee)
Craig Hays (USA, Designee)
Lee Dong Gyu (Korea, Designee) In support: **Choi Eui-Sun (Korea),**
Francisco Blotta (Argentina, Designee)
Cesar Rodriguez (Iceland, Designee)
Ramiro Guzman (Mexico, Designee) represented by Proxy

Current World Moo Duk Kwan Country Designees Appointed by the Kwan Jang Nim

Leonardo Barboza Rodríguez. Dan Bon: 47553 Costa Rica
Gil Won Lee Dan Bon: 3759 Korea
Edgardo Grandeza Dan Bon: 12197 Philippines
Ramiro Guzman Dan Bon: 16354 Mexico
Young Ho Lee Dan Bon: 16889 New Zealand
Francisco Blotta Dan Bon: 19455 Argentina
Xavier Dufour. Dan Bon : 36706 Belgium
Gianni Anile Chiarelli Dan Bon: 21328 Italy
Kostas Papadopoulos Dan Bon: 21542 Greece
Thian Lok Lim Dan Bon: 23321 Malaysia
Moshe Jakobi Dan Bon: 23640 Israel
Kriton Glenn, Dan Bon: 23757 Australia
Elodie Mollet Dan Bon: 38935 France
Urs Spoerri Dan Bon: 26021 Switzerland
Frank Schnitzler Dan Bon: 47551 Germany
Diego Salinas Dan Bon: 35919 Spain
Cesar Rodriguez Luna Dan Bon: 44158 Iceland
Robert Hedges Dan Bon: 22420 UK/Ireland
Alex Carrillo Sanhueza Dan Bon: 34686 Chile
Roberto Fontora Dan Bon: 34127 Uruguay
Craig Hays Dan Bon: 23132 USA
Mostafa Mahmoudi Dan Bon: 32958 Iran
Jim Class Dan Bon: #35373 Puerto Rico

Possible pending New designees:
Brazil – Mr. Fabiano Mello Dan Bon: 42480
Panama – Mr. Geovani Ernesto Padiila Arauz Dan Bon: 42479

2018

March 2018

March 16-18: Attended the Region 10, 141st Dan Shim Sa and the TAC tour in Seattle, WA.

March 23-25: Attended the Region 5, 141st Dan Shim Sa and the TAC tour in Illinois.

April 2018

2018 April :7th: Attended the Region 2 141st Dan Shim Sa at NY State

2018 April: 13th -14th: Attended the Region 9 141st Dan Shim Sa & T.A.C. tour at Lomita Park, CA

2018 April 20-23rd: Attended the 141st Dan Shim Sa and Sa Bom Clinics, Seoul, Korea

May 2018

2018 May 4th -5th: Attended the Region 3 141st Dan Shim Sa and T.A.C. tour, Myrtle Beach, SC

2018 May 12th: Attended the Region 2 T.A.C. tour, Springfield, NJ

2018 May 18th -19th: Attended the Region 6 T.A.C. tour, Houston, TX

July 2018

2018 July 28th –August 4th: Attended the Euro Summer Camp, Switzerland

August 2018

2018 August 9th -12th: Attended the 40th U.S. Nationals Festival & World Moo Duk Kwan 12th Designees Zone Symposium, Houston, TX

2018 August 12th: Presents the NEW World T. A.C. members:
Ramiro Guzman Sa Bom Nim Dan Bon: Dan Bon:16354 Mexico
Donggyu Lee Sa Bom Nim Dan Bon: 16863 Korea
Daymon Kenyon Sa Bom Nim Dan Bon: 19839 U.S.A
Diego Salinas Sa Bom Nim Dan Bon:35919 Spain

September 2018

2018 September 15th: Historic meeting of Past Moo Duk Kwan Members from Soo Bahk Do, Tang Soo Do and Tae Kwon Do to re-establish their connection to the Moo Duk Kwan through the New World Moo Duk Kwan Heritage Membership Program.
The meeting was attended by:
Kwan Jang Nim H.C. Hwang
Frank Bonsigore, Fred Scott, Larry Seiberlich, Darryl Khalid, Joe Goss, Charles Ferrero, Wesley C. Jenkins, Mar DiScipio, Daymon Kenyon, Tom Wasylyk, Stuart Tierney, Keith J. Bennett, Ricka Rubems, Carmela Fox, Cort Stinehour, Samuel Wallace, Andy Leonard, Guy Petroski, Steve Voelker, Stephane Huguier, Frank Tsai, David Kremin, Rich Kopf, Don Straga, Joe Gross Jr., Dominick Giacobbe, Erica Tierney, John Trudgill.

September 21-23rd: Attended the Region 4, 142nd Dan Shim Sa and TAC tour, Viera, Florida.

September 28th -29th: Attended the Region 8 142nd Dan Shim Sa and T.A.C. tour, Salt Lake City, UT.

October 2018

October 11th -15th: 10th Attended the SEALS (South East Asia Leadership Seminars), Melbourne, Australia.

October 19th -25th: Conducted the 17th Korean Ko Dan Ja Shim Sa and attended the 3rd WMDK Youth Leader Symposium, Kang Hwa island, Korea

November 2018

November 9th -16th: Conducted the U.S.A. 35th Ko Dan Ja Shim Sa, Houston. TX

November 30th –December 2nd: Attended: Greece 50th years anniversary of Moo Duk Kwan, Athens, Greece.

2019

Began his 65th anniversary year of training in the Moo Duk Kwan

April 2019

April 12th – 14th: Conduct Sa Bom seminars at the Central Do Jang in Yong San, Korea.

April 13th: The 143rd Dan Classing Shim Sa at Central Do Jang in Yong San, Korea.

April 14th: Conduct Seminars for members of the Korean Soo Bahk Do Moo Duk Kwan.

April 27th-28th: Attended UK open Tang Soo Do tournament, Cardiff, Wales Hosted by Master John Trudgill and conducted seminar and World Moo Duk Kwan Heritage Membership Program. Task force members: Fred Scott,(Dan # 19187) Steve Voelker, (Dan#22632) John Trudgill.(Dan#26146), Dennis Leonard (Dan#22919), Erica Tieney, Cort Stinehour (Dan#33190), Frank Tsai,(Dan#32700) and Steven Diaz (Dan#19461)

May 2019

May 29th – June 4th: Conducted the 10th Euro Ko Dan Ja Shim Sa, Evia Island, Greece

June 2019

June 1st: Released 75th anniversary collectors edition of the Founder Hwang Kee's Soo Bahk Do (Tang Soo Do) Vol. 1

June 15th: Attended: Jion Hyung Masters Clinic, hosted by Master Frederick Scott and the Traditional Tang Soo Do International. Supporting members included: Frank Bonsignore Sa Bom Nim (Dan#15805), Russell Colston Sa Bom Nim (Dan#22358), Frank Tsai Sa Bom Nim (Dan#32700). and Cort Stinehour Sa Bom Nim (Dan#33190)

July 2019

July 25th-27th: Attended the 40th U.S. Nationals Festival, Portland, Oregon

July 27th: promoted the ***first Kyo-Boms*** at the U.S. National Festival, Portland, Oregon
George Broyles, Robert Siegel, Doug Countryman, Matthew Wyatt and Sean Oulashin
This is a historic moment for our Art. Prior to the Korean War, our Founder Hwang Kee was the only Sa Bom an instructors were Kyo Sa (usually under the rank of Dan) and Kyo Bom. After the Korean War instructors were K Sa's (Dan members) and Sa Bom's
The term of Kyo Bom was not used after the war. There are 2 reasons that the term Kyo Bom is reintroduced. 1) To certify Sa Dan's that choose not to be an instructor yet be certified to teach and promote students at Gup level. 2) Younger practitioners (21 - 24) have a proper title and certification. Giving them a place to be proud of their connection, rank and position. Kyo Bom meets our 5 Moo Do Values (History, tradition, Philosophy, Discipline/ Respect and Technique) and will add value by elevating our Sa Bom Nim's

2019

August 2019

August 10th, presented the Moo Duk Kwan Heritage seminar at an event hosted by Master Dominick Giacobbe ir Atlantic City, NJ

August 10th Attended a meeting of the Moo Duk Kwan Heritage task force. In attendance were:
Master Dominick Giacobbe (Dan#18656), Master John Trudgill (Dan#26146)
Master Steve Voelker (Dan#22632), Master Fred Scott (Dan#18187), Master Erica Scott Tiernet, Master Cort Stinehour, (Dan#33190), Master Steve Diaz,(Dan#19461) ,Master Andy Leonard (Dan#22919),Master Frank Tsa (Dan#32700)

October 2019

October 5th attended the WDU/USG National Championships in Norwich Connecticut

October 17th Attend the Heritage meeting with Masters Jong H Lee and Matt Hugh who represent one of Tae Kwon Do group.

October 18th 24th conducted the 18th Korea Ko Dan Ja Shim Sa and the 4th WMDK Youth Leader Symposium at the Kyei Myung Training Center in Kang Hwa Island, Korea.

October 26th Conducted the 144th Dan Test and presented the Moo Duk Kwan Heritage program at the Central Do Jang in Yong San, Korea.

November 2019
November 8th-10th, attended the U.S. Moment with the Masters, Midway, Utah
November 8th- 15th, conducted the U.S.A. 36th Ko Dan Ja Shim Sa, Midway, Utah

December 2019
December 9th-12th, attended the World Moo Duk Kwan Designee's symposium, Mendoza, Argentina
December 6th -13th, conducted the South American (WMDK Zone 4) Ko Dan Ja Shim Sa, Mendoza, Argentina

December 14, The 2019 National Moo Do Festival as a celebration of the 45th years of Moo Duk Kwan in Argentina

2020

Begins his 66th anniversary year of training in the Moo Duk Kwan

January 8: Russ Hanke Sa Bom Nim's (Dan#4137,Charter member, S.A.C.) passing

January 9: Visit to Detroit for the final bow with Hanke Sa Bom Nim

January 12: Meeting with Moo Duk Kwan alumni Masters Kong, Sin Young (447), John Natividad (14435), Darnell Garcia (14475), and his students to support the WMDK Heritage Program.
January 15: Conducts Sip Dan Khum Hyung clinic at the South Bay Moo Duk Kwan in Torrance, CA. 7th Dan award ceremony for George Dolby Sa Bom (19028).

February
February 8th-9th, attended and conducted a Moo Duk Kwan Heritage event at the Holiday Inn Bolton Centre, U.K. for members from the U.K. and Ireland.

February 9th, conducted a clinic for Ko Dan Ja members from U.K., U.S.A, Spain and France.

March
March 1st: Conducted a training session for several members of the Guardian of the Art at headquarters in Spring Field, NJ. In attendance were Sa Bom Nim's, H.Y. Kwon (Dan# 10805), Benjamin Cortese (Dan #11689),Frank Bonsignore (Dan # 15805), Russell Colston (Dan #22538)

March 4th, celebrates his 73rd birthday

2020

March 2020
The world is struck with the COVID19 Pandemic. This global event altered the planned events worldwide for the Moo Duk Kwan as well as all members and their families.

April 12th,
Understanding the effects of this global situation Kwan Jang Nim H.C. Hwang sets in motion a series of weekly instructional videos to further assist and connect members around the globe through social media. The topics covered were: the use of the huri, fundamental Cha Gi's and the importance of the eight key concepts. Also included were historical videos of the Founder, his personal growth and the original Dojang

May 4th, recognizes 14 Early Moo Duk Kwan Pioneers through the World Moo Duk Kwan Heritage Program: Those pioneers acknowledged were:

- Dale Drouillard (Dan#757)
- Mariano Estioko (Dan#759)
- Robert Thompson (1791)
- Lawrence Seiberlich (Dan# 1815)
- John Butterwick (Dan# 2277)
- Robert Cheezic (Dan# 2278)
- Chuck Norris (Dan#2819)
- Joe Weeks (Dan #3596)
- Lynn Jackson (Dan # 3597)
- David Praim (Dan # 3593)
- Russell Hanke (Dan #4137)
- Robert Shipley (Dan# 4825)
- Robert Beaudoin (Dan#5657)
- Robert Sohn (Dan#6037)

May 9th: Conducts ,World Moo Duk Kwan TAC Clinic & Meeting at 5PM EST.
R Guzman (16354), Dong Kyu Lee (16863), Daymon Kenyon (19839), and Diego Salinas (35919) attended.
May 13th, begins sharing the Moo Duk Kwan' history though the World Moo Duk Kwan Heritage program in a series of videos through social media through July.
May 15th, Announced the postponed event for the 75th Anniversary;

"I hope you and your families are well. As we continue to endure the global crisis of the CORVID 1 pandemic, it has become apparent that a return to normal activity and previously scheduled events is still i the distant future. For this reason I have made the decision to postpone the 75th Anniversary of the Moo Duk Kwan celebration scheduled for this October in Seoul, Korea. Personal, social, and economic hardship have created an environment requiring all of us to re-purpose our lives and essential activities toward our health, recovery, and stabilization.
The new tentative dates are as follows: October 19-25 2021 (Ko Dan Ja Shim Sa, Kae Myung Facility, Ganghwa Island) October 25-27 2021 , 75th Anniversary of the Moo Duk Kwan celebration (Same hotel venue as previously announced). For those who have already committed financially to this year's event, return reimbursements will be fully honored. It is my hope and sincere wish to see you all safely through th time of hardship, and to join me and the Moo Duk Kwan family in Seoul next year. My best wishes for you during this difficult time.
Sincerely, H.C Hwang, President, World Moo Duk Kwan"

May 16th: Conducts World Moo Duk Kwan TAC Clinic & Meeting

May 23rd: Conducts World Moo Duk Kwan TAC Clinic & Meeting

May 30th: Conducts World Moo Duk Kwan TAC Clinic & Meeting

June

June12th: PDT (Project Delivery Team) was formed for preparing the 75th Virtual Celebration of Moo Duk Kwan.

Steve Diaz, Chair person (19461), Frank Tsai (32700), Eui Sun Choi (19203), DK Chang (20780), Cort Stinehour (33190), Jared Rosenthal (32740), Brian Corrales (36364), Robert Hedges (22420), Diego Salinas (35919), Steve Voelker (22632), Ricardo Giorgi (27516), Lauren Brotherton (38008), Stephen LeHars (45754), Kim Wyles (33986), Elodie Mollet (38935), Sean Oulashin (44504), Francisco R Blotta (29030), Steven Lemner (23703) and Tim McHugh.

June 13th: Conducts Virtual class with US TAC, and World Moo Duk Kwan TAC Clinic & Meeting

June 20th: PDT meeting and conducts World Moo Duk Kwan TAC Clinic & Meeting

June 27th: Conducts World Moo Duk Kwan TAC Clinic & Meeting

June 30th: New appointment for TAC and TAC assistants in Mexico
New TAC members Elizabeth Mora (Dan#31626) to Neh Gong Bu, Anthony K. Guzman (Dan#42874) to Weh Gong Bu, and New TAC assistants: Francisco Ramírez (Dan#44836),
Lorena Cortés (Dan#45396), Jaime Ambriz (Dan#47524)

July

July 3rd: Conducted WMDK Zone 4 (South America zone) Virtual seminar

July 11th: PDT meeting to plan the 75th virtual celebration

July 14th: The founder Hwang Kee's 18th memorial service

July 18th: Conducted World Moo Duk Kwan TAC Clinic & Meeting

July 19th, Announcement about the Moo Duk Kwan® 75th Virtual Anniversary Celebration to be held from the beginning of October 2020 to November 9th, 2020.

PDT discussed to prepare a daily drift campaign during the month of October. Producing videos from each country for the drift campaign and basic guidelines to include in the video was discussed

July 25th: Conducted WMDK Youth Leader's Virtual seminars and World Moo Duk Kwan TAC Clinic

August

August 1st: PDT and Assist Sip Dan Khum #6 Seminars by the US TAC chair (Craig Hayes Dan # 23132)

August 7th: PDT Meeting

August 15th: Assist Sip Dan Khum #7 Seminars by the US TAC chair (Craig Hayes Dan # 23132)at and conduct World Moo Duk Kwan TAC Clinic & Meeting

August 22nd: Assist Sip Dan Khum #8 seminars by the US TAC chair (Craig Hayes Dan # 23132) and conduits World Moo Duk Kwan TAC Clinic & Meeting

August 29th: Assist Sip Dan Khum #9 seminars by the US TAC chair (Craig Hayes Dan # 23132) and conduits World Moo Duk Kwan TAC Clinic & Meeting

September

September 1st: **US TAC re appointment was made for the next 3 years term.**
Technical (Ki Sul Bu), Jeff Griggs (Dan # 23269), Jen Gibbons (Dan #32238)
Digital Media (Digital Bu),Frank Tsai SBN(Dan # 32700), Brian Corrales (Dan# 36364)
MDK Preservation (Jin Heung Bu),Cort Stinehour (Dan #33190) Jared Rosenthal (Dan # 32740)
Administration (Heng Jeung Bu) Josh Lockwood (Dan # 29755), Michael Zickafoose (Dan#30699)
TAC Chairman, Craig Hays (Dan# 23132)
TAC Assistants, Rodrigo Cruz (Dan# 33484) (Technical & Digital Media), (Technical & Digital Media),Josh Duncan (Dan# 29793) (Technical),Sue Fittanto (Dan#41586) (Digital Media & Preservation),Master Ed Horni (Dan#36429) (Administration)

September 5th: Assist Sip Dan Khum #10 seminars by the US TAC chair and Conducted World Moo Duk Kwan TAC Clinic & Meeting.

September 12th: Conducted World Moo Duk Kwan TAC Clinic & Meeting.

September 14th: Australian TAC reappointment was made for the next 3 years term. Sa Bom Nim Mark Koina (Dan #34683), Kim Wyles (Dan # 33986)

September 19th: PDT meeting

September 20th, announces the agenda for the 75th Moo Duk Kwan Virtual celebration, with live virtual clinics to be conducted by himself for opening and closing ceremonies for the global membership, and clinic from the four zones, conducted by the World Moo Duk Kwan T.A.C. members: Those members were:
Zone 1: Sa Bom Nim Dong Gyu Lee (Dan# 16863) (Korea)
Zone 2: Sa Bom Nim Daymon Kenyon (Dan#19839)(USA)
Zone 3: Sa Bom Nim Diego Salinas (Dan#35919) (Spain)
Zone 4: Sa Bom Nim Ramiro Guzman (Dan# 16354) (Mexico)

September 26th: Conducted World Moo Duk Kwan TAC Clinic & Meeting.

October

October: authorizes and approves the release of videos to begin the celebration for the 75th Virtual celebration, with historic videos of countries from around the globe, demonstrations, senior members interviews to be shared on social media platforms.

October 17th, attended the first Virtual USA National Championships. The USA T.A.C., T.A.C. assistants , Regional examiners and other trained virtual competition officials are currently working through judging all the excellent performances submitted by members nationwide.

"Kwan Jang Nim H.C. Hwang has commended Federation Officials for the amazing success of this event.

Dear Virtual Festival Officials,

I hope this message finds you and your family safe and well.

Your creative solution for hosting a meaningful National Festival experience for members under the current conditions is greatly appreciated. Excellent member participation indicates that they were very excited about the experience you provided for them. I too, am excited to see the TAC, TAC Assistants, Board, Regional Examiners and selected members working together harmoniously for our common goal and for the preservation of our art. Your use of modern technology to overcome obstacles facing Moo Duk Kwan members is impressive. The Moo Duk Kwan was born amidst very challenging post war circumstances in Korea and yet our Founder persevered against all odds.

I am glad to see his spirit exhibited today by the Federation's leadership. Thank you very much for adding this very successful event to the long list of Moo Duk Kwan achievements.

In Moo Duk Kwan, H.C. Hwang"

October 3rd: PDT meeting

October 10th: Conducted WMDK Youth Leader and Senior Advisory Team for YL virtual seminars and World Moo Duk Kwan TAC Clinic & Meeting.

October 20th, appointed the first panel of members to the inaugural Sa Jei Ji Gahn Committee dedicated to the long-term preservation of harmonious relations among Soo Bahk Do® practitioners and Instructors.

Those members are Sa Bom Nim's

- Lawrence Seiberlich (Dan# 1815), USA
- Kriton Glenn (Dan#23757), Australia
- Maria Del Pilar Guzman (Dan#22013), Mexico
- Ricardo Giorgi (Dan#27516), Argentina
- Diego Salinas (Dan# 35919),Spain

Sa Jei Ji Gahn is defined as:

- Sa - referring to Sa Bom
- Jei - referring to the Jei Ja ranking system (student/disciple)
- Ji Gahn - referring to the relationship between Instructor and Student

Seeking to avoid conflict is an essential characteristic valued by those who embrace the cultural, philosophical and Moo Do attributes that Founder Hwang Kee infused into his martial art system and which make it unique.

This Committee will consider and provide recommendations to the World Moo Duk Kwan (WMDK) for resolution of relationship issues as encountered on a national and international basis. The Committee will consider only those issues that have not been successfully resolved by the World Moo Duk Kwan's extensive existing structure.

October 24th: PDT meeting at 10:30AM EST. World Moo Duk Kwan TAC Clinic & Meeting.

October 31st: PDT rehearsal meeting for the 75th

November

November 4th: PDT rehearsal meeting

November 5th: PDT rehearsal meeting

November 6th, **Conducts the opening ceremonies and hosts a international clinic via social media. He presented a historical video of the Founder Hwang Kee and the Moo Duk Kwan.**

November 8th: PDT meeting

November 9th, **Conducts the closing ceremonies and host an international clinic via social media, with histological videos.**

1. Video recognizing the pioneers of the Moo Duk Kwan
2. Video recognizing the Significant Contributors to the Moo Duk Kwan from around the globe

Criteria: -

A. Consistent dedication to the Moo Duk Kwan under the Founder's leadership

B. Moo Duk Kwan issued Dan Bon (under 24,000)

C. Use of Moo Duk Kwan Do Bok

D. Studio Owner, Tournament Competitor or other significant contribution

3. The World Moo Duk Kwan Heritage Program and its task force.

4. Video recognizing the World Moo Duk Kwan Heritage Significant Contributors from Tae Kwon Do.

    A. Certified by the Founder Hwang Kee

    B. Moo Duk Kwan issued Dan Bon

    C. Contributed to the spread of the Moo Duk Kwan legacy through Tae Kwon Do outside of Korea.

5. Video recognizing the World Moo Duk Kwan Heritage Significant Contributors from Tang Soo Do.

A. Certified by the Founder Hwang Kee

    B. Moo Duk Kwan issued Dan Bon

    C. Contributed to the spread of the Moo Duk Kwan legacy through Tang Soo Do outside of Korea.

November 14th: Conducted World Moo Duk Kwan TAC Clinic & Meeting

November 15th: WMDK Heritage Program Task Force meeting

November 21st: Conducted All National TAC with the WMDK TAC seminars

December

December 5th: Conducted WMDK Youth Leader seminars

December 12th: Conducted World Moo Duk Kwan TAC Clinic & Meeting **(2020 Year end gathering)**

December 19th: Conducted All National TAC with the WMDK TAC final clinic in 2020

Sa Bom Nim Russell Hanke
Gu Dan, 4137, Region 5
S.A.C. Member
U.S. Soo Bahk Do® (Tang Soo Do) Moo Duk Kwan®
founding member

Sa Bom Nim Russ Hanke's History:
1960's

(The following was researched by Steven Lemner Sa Bom Nim student of Russ Hanke Sa Bom Nim with the help of Kwan Jang Nim H.C. Hwang, Romero Guzman Sa Bom Nim, Josh Lockwood Sa Bom Nim and Michael Zickafoose Sa Bom Nim. All Ranking was authorized by the Moo Duk Kwan ® Organization, and it's founder Hwang Kee and Kwan Jang Nim H.C. Hwang and he is fully certified in the Soo Bahk Do ® martial art style and tang soo do. It is with honor his martial arts time line is presented.)

Born: 8/26/1940 in Detroit, Michigan
Parents: Mother: Anne Amend. Deceased , Father: Louis Hanke. Deceased, with two siblings: One sister, one brother
He has two children, Two sons, Brett, and Shane

1960: Started training in the Moo Duk Kwan at YMCA in Wyandotte, MI. (under Dale Drouillard, Dan Bon 757)

1960-1962: Returning servicemen and others begin opening Tang Soo Do studios in U.S. including:

Dale Drouilard (#757) in Wyandotte, Michigan

Lawrence Seiberlich(#1815) in St. Paul Min.

Robert Cheezic (#2278) Waterbury, CT.

Frank Trojanowicz (#13333)

Lynn Jackson(#3597) Oberlin, Ohio

Russell Hanke(#4137)Detroit Mich.

James Cummings(#4493)Military

David J. Praim(#3593), Mt. Clemems, MI.

Jong Hyan Lee (#1885), San Diego Ca.

Robert Thompson(#1791) in Dayton Ohio

John Butterwick(#2277)Military

Carlos 'Chuck' Norris (#2819),Torrance Ca.

Joe Weeks(#3596),Magnolia Ar.

James Ruston(#4130) Military

Robert Sohn (#6037) New York.

Robert Shipley(#4825), Honolulu Hi

Robert Beaudoin (#5657) Waterbury, CT.

Lynn Jackson (#3597) Lorain Ohio

Ki Whang Kim (No Dan Bon) (Washington D.C.) Shim Sang Kyu(#180) Wyandotte, Mi.

Ahn Kyong Won (#1763) Cincinnati, OH

1961: Promoted to 1st Dan (Dan Bon 4137) (Under Master Sang Kyu Shim)

1963: Started teaching at the YMCA (Taught there until 1967)

1963: Promoted to 2nd Dan (under Master Sang Kyu Shim)

1963: Sponsored Sang Kyu Shim to the United States as Kwan Jang Nim Hwang Kee's emissary. (Sang Kyu Shim lived with him for 9 months)

1966: Promoted to 3rd Dan (Under Master Lee)

1970's

1970: Promoted to 4th Dan (Under Master Drouillard)
1974: Hosted the first United States clinic by Kwan Jang Nim Hwang Kee (held in Lincoln Park, MI.) First time the Moo Pahl Dan Khum and Moon Pahl Dan Khum were introduced. Russ Hanke Sa Bom Nim has lead these at all future Ko Dan Ja Shim Sa's, international. national and regional, summer camps, until becoming a S.A.C. member in 1999.
1974: Accepted by Kwan Jang Nim H.C. Hwang as his student
1975: Participated in the Charter Convention and was established as one of the founding members (Charter Member) of the U.S. Soo Bahk Do (Tang Soo Do)Moo Duk Kwan Federation

1974 October: Attended: United States Soo Bahk Do Moo Duk Kwan directors convention and general meeting of all USA members at Burlington, NJ

The Task Force Members were: (Sa Boms /Masters and other)

1. Jae Chul Shin (#698) 2. Robert Thompson(#1791) 3. Tchang Bok Chung (#12641) 4. Chuck Blackburn (#12197) 5. Arthur Fontaine (#14350) 6. Joe Weeks (#3696) 7. Andy Ahpo (#10187), and Charles di Pierro. *Officers of the first Board of Directors, of the U.S. Tang Soo Do Moo Duk Kwan Federation™ were:*

Kwan Jang Nim Hwang Kee, President, Hyun Chul Hwang(#509) TAC Chairman, Charles di Pierro, Chairman of Board, Victor Martinov (#10189), Vice Chairman of Board, Andy Ah Po (#10187), Secretary , Arthur Pryor (16505),Treasurer

Additional members of the board were: Chun Sik Kim (#2457) ***, Russ Hanke (#4137),*** Frank Trojanowicz (#13333), Robert Shipley (#4825), Lynn Jackson (#3597) , Robert Kingsley (#6044), Tchang -Bok Chung (#12641), Joe Weeks (#3596), Larry Seiberlich (#1815), Jeff Moonitz (#17650), Fred Kenyon (#14345), Bob Beaudoin (#5661), Ben Cortese (#11689), Frank Bonsignore (#15805), Dennis Miller (#18430), Ronald Savage (#15879), Lyn Stanwich, James Lee (#14317)

1975 June 28th: Attended: United States Soo Bahk Do Charter convention and special seminar by Grandmaster Hwang Kee (Hilton Hotel, NY)

The Charter was ratified making this event the **official birth of the Federation**.

Those in attendance were: (Sa Boms/Masters/Dans) Kwan Jang Nim Hwang Kee, Hyun Chul Hwang (#509), Chun Sik Kim (#2457), Yong Ki Hong (#4142), Andy Ah Po (#10187), Carl Jenkins (#18983), Ronald Savage (#15879), Dennis E. Miller (#18430), Peter Canciani (#18911), Warren Adams, Jeff Moonitz (#17650), Frank Trojanowicz (#13333), Paul Johnson, Frank Bonsignore (#15805), Arthur Pryor (#16505), Benjamin Cortese (#11689), Larry Seiberlich (#1815), Robert Fernandez, Jr. (#17927), Robert Fernandez, Sr. (#14464), Joe Weeks (#3596), Ki Yul Yu (#5311), Holly A. Whitehouse (#18943), James N. Rushton, Victor Martinov (#10189), Fred Kenyon (#14345), Joyce M. Keyes (#19448), ***Russell Hanke (#4137),*** Robert Beaudoin (#5661), Robert Rondelli (#17416), Psyche Harry Smith (#18143), James Lee (#14317), Greg William (#11695), Robert Shipley (#4825)

1975: Promoted to 5th Dan (Under Kwan Jang Nim Hwang Kee)
1976: Appointed as Board Member by Kwan Jang Nim Hwang Kee

1978: Attended: 1st U.S. Tang Soo Do Moo Duk Kwan Nationals-7-22-78 Concord Hotel NY
1978: Established Russ Hanke's Capture, Contain, Control system and instructed to police and sheriffs departments in Michigan.
1978: Developed Nutcracker Flails (a form of Nunchaku) for police and sheriffs departments in Michiga
1979: October 26-28, Attended: U.S. National Convention for Ho Sin Sool / Hyungs standardization

1980's

1980: Attended 2nd U.S. Tang Soo Do Moo Duk Kwan Nationals, 3-22-80, Pittsburg, PA.
1981: Promoted to 6th Dan (Under Kwan Jang Nim Hwang Kee)
1981: Attended 3rd U.S. Tang Soo Do Moo Duk Kwan Nationals, 4-11-81 Roselle, NJ
1982: Attended 4th U.S. Tang Soo Do Moo Duk Kwan Nationals, 11-21-82 Atlantic City, NJ (Internationals 11-20-82)

1983: August, Attended The 2nd Chil Song Hyung clinic by the founder. Kang Uk Lee (70), W.Y. Chung(410), C.I. Kim (475), H.C. Hwang (509), and C.S.Kim (2457) were attended.

1983: December 4th-7th: Attended: The 1st U.S. Ko Dan Ja Shim Sa (for 4 days) at Springfield, NJ. Candidates were; Lloyd Francis (14500), Larry Jones (15849) Ron Cehner (18450), Patrick Jorgensen (18934), Daniel Nolan (19035), and Russ Hanke (4137) as an official.

1983: Attended 5th U.S. Tang Soo Do Moo Duk Kwan Nationals, 11-5-83 San Diego, CA
1984: Attended 6th U.S. Tang Soo Do Moo Duk Kwan Nationals, 10-27-84 West Point, NY

1984: December 3rd-7th: Attended: The 2nd U.S. Ko Dan Ja Shim Sa at the Springfield Headquarters Do Jang in NJ. Candidates were; Larry Seiberlich (1815), Ben Cortese (11689), Jeff Moonitz (17650), Fred Scott (19187), and Russ Hanke (4137) as an official.

1985: Attended 7th U.S. Tang Soo Do Moo Duk Kwan Nationals, 11-22-85 Anaheim, CA

1986: Attended 8th U.S. Tang Soo Do Moo Duk Kwan Nationals, 11-21-86 Stamford, CN

1986: November 1986: Participated in the 3rd U.S. Ko Dan Ja Shim Sa at Springfield Headquarters, Do Jang in NJ. It was the first full 8 days of Shim Sa at the new headquarters Do Jang in NJ. Candidates were; Andy Ahpo (10187), Victor Martinov (10189), Wilton Bennett, Jr. (19027), Frank Schermerhorn (19787), Don Southerton (19192), Charlie Ferraro (19986), Yeon Seo (20564), Philip Bartolacci (20571), and Russ Hanke (4137)

1987: July: Attended: Special International Summer Camp Training at Pathwork Center, NY

1987: Attended: 9th U.S. Tang Soo Do Moo Duk Kwan Nationals, 11-13-87 Bal Harbor, FL

1987: Attended 4th Ko Dan Ja Shim Sa, U.S.A. Headquarters, Springfield, NJ.

1988: Attended: 10th U.S. Tang Soo Do Moo Duk Kwan Nationals, 10-28-88 West Point NY

1988: Promoted to 7th Dan (Under Kwan Jang Nim Hwang Kee)
1988: November: Attended: The 5th Ko Dan Ja Shim Sa, U.S.A., at headquarters Dojang, Springfield, NJ.

1988: Attended seminars at Winter Camp, (Yuk Ro Hyung) Homestead, FL.

1989: July : Attended: International Summer Camp at the Pathwalk Center, NY

1989: January: Attended Ko Dan Ja meeting with the Founder, Hwang Kee, who initiates discussion of "Mission 2000" agenda.

1989: Attended 11th U.S. Tang Soo Do Moo Duk Kwan Nationals, 10-13-89 Anaheim, CA

1989: Candidate at: October, attended 6th Ko Dan Ja Shim Sa, U.S.A. ,Springfield, NJ.

1990's

1990: July: Attended International Summer Camp at the Pathwalk Center, NY

1990: Attended 12th U.S. Tang Soo Do Moo Duk Kwan Nationals, 10-5-90 Concord Hotel, NY
1990: Attended 7th Ko Dan Ja Shim Sa, U.S.A. ,Springfield, NJ

1991: Attended 13th U.S. Tang Soo Do Moo Duk Kwan Nationals, 11-1-91 Bonaventure Hotel, FL
1991: March: Appointed to the Technical Advisory Committee:

The first U.S. TAC Committee members were appointed by the Founder. They were; Sa Boms Nim's / .L. Seiberlich (1810), Russ Hanke (4137), S.D. Cho (8013), Y.K. Hong (9193), A. Ahpo (10187), and V. Martinov (10189)

1991: March: Attended: 1st Yuk Ro Hyung clinic for newly appointed U.S. TAC members at the headquarters Do Jang in Springfield, NJ

1991: July: Attended: Yuk Ro Hyung Clinics for the U.S. Regional Examiners at the Summer Camp, Owaisa Bauer, FL.

1991: Attended 8th Ko Dan Ja Shim Sa, U.S.A. , Springfield, NJ.

1991: Re-Appointed as Regional Examiner to Region 5 following reorganization of U.S. Federation into (10 Regions.)
1991: Attended 1st Yuk Ro Hyung Clinic (Under Kwan Jang Nim Hwang Kee)

1992: Attended 14th U.S. Tang Soo Do Moo Duk Kwan Nationals, 10-23-92 Ft. Lauderdale, FL

1992: August: International Summer Camp at the Pathwalk Center, NY

1992: Attended 9th Ko Dan Ja Shim Sa, U.S.A. ,Springfield, NJ.

1993: July: Attended: International Summer Camp in Connecticut.

1993: Attended 15th U.S. Tang Soo Do Moo Duk Kwan Nationals, 10-15-93 Dallas, TX
1993: Attended International Clinics and Demonstrations (Greece)

1993: Attended 10th Ko Dan Ja Shim Sa, U.S.A. , Springfield, NJ.

1994: Kwan Jang Nim H.C. Hwang begins the "Instructional Guides" National Tour, to promote New Gup Instructional Guide books to membership for increased standardization. Sa Bom Nim Hanke authored Vol.1 Soo Bahk Do /Tang Soo Do Dae Kham) Study Guide used for Dan Testing candidates at this time.

1994: June: Attended: International Summer Camp at the Pathwalk Center, NY

1994: Attended:16th U.S. Tang Soo Do Moo Duk Kwan Nationals, 9-9-94 San Diego, CA

1994:*11th Ko Dan Ja Shim Sa, U.S.A. ,Springfield, NJ.* ***(last time the Founder, Kwan Jang Nim Hwang Kee attended a Ko Dan Ja in the U.S.A.)***

1995: January**:** Founder sponsored Technical Advisory Committee meeting, San Diego, California
1995: Attended:17th U.S. Soo Bahk Do (Tang Soo Do) Moo Duk Kwan Nationals, 6-23-95 Orlando, FL
1995: Attended: 50th Anniversary of the Moo Duk Kwan (Seoul, Korea)
1995: Attended, 12th Ko Dan Ja Shim Sa, U.S.A. ,Springfield, NJ

1995: July**:** Attended: International Summer Camp at the Pathwalk Center, NY

1996: Attended:18th U.S. Soo Bahk Do (Tang Soo Do) Moo Duk Kwan Nationals, 8-2-96 San Diego, C
1996: Attended 13th Ko Dan Ja Shim Sa, U.S.A., Springfield, NJ

1996:July 18-20: Attended: International Summer Camp at the Pathwalk Center in Phoenicia, NY

1996: August 3rd: ***Tang Soo Do Moo Duk Kwan Federation Inc. changed it's name to the U.S. Soo Bahk Do Moo Duk Kwan Federation Inc.***

1997: July: 16th~20th of July visited: Guadalajara, Mexico

1997: Attended: 19th U.S. Soo Bahk Do (Tang Soo Do) Moo Duk Kwan Nationals, 8-15-97 Cherry Hill, NJ. TAC Demonstrations / 1st Public Demonstration of Chil Sung Yuk Ro Hyung.

1997: Attended 14th Ko Dan Ja Shim Sa, U.S.A. ,Springfield, NJ.

1998: May 29th-31st: Attended the U.S National clinics for Chil Song / Yuk Ro Hyung in San Diego, CA

1998: June 26th-28th: Attended: International Summer Camp at the Pathwalk Center in Phoenicia, NY

1998: Attended 15th Ko Dan Ja Shim Sa, U.S.A. ,Springfield, NJ.

1998: Attended:20th U.S. Soo Bahk Do (Tang Soo Do) Moo Duk Kwan Nationals, 7-31-98 Cincinnati, OH. This is the first time Region 5 hosted a U.S. Soo Bahk Do Nationals.

1999: Attended: 16th Ko Dan Ja Shim Sa, Springfield , NJ.
1999: Attended: 21st U.S. Soo Bahk Do (Tang Soo Do) Moo Duk Kwan Nationals, 7-30-99 Houston, TX
1999: Appointed to the Senior Advisory Committee (at this time he stopped teaching the Moo Pahl Dan Kyum at events, allowing others to carry it on)

January 1st: The 1st Senior Advisory Committee (SAC) was appointed by the Founder. They were: Sa Bom Nim's:

W.Y. Chung (410), L. Seiberlich (1815),R. Hanke (4137),A. Ahpo (10187) and

V. Martinov (10189)

1999 January 1st: The 2nd generations of the US TAC members were appointed by the founder. They were: Sa Bom Nim's:

Robert Shipley (4825) – Neh Gong Bu

Ted Mason (112895) – Neh Gong Bu

Frank Bonsignore (15805) – Neh Gong Bu

Frank Schermerhorn (19787) – Weh Gong Bu

Daymon Kenyon (19839) – Weh Gong Bu

Philip Bartolacci (20571) – Weh Gong Bu

Hyuk Woon Kwon (10805) – Shim Gong Bu

Jeff Moonitz (17650) – Shim Gong Bu

Mary Ann Walsh (17926) – Shim Gong Bu

1999: Promoted to 8th Dan (Under Kwan Jang Nim Hwang Kee)

2000's

2000: Attended:22nd U.S. Soo Bahk Do (Tang Soo Do) Moo Duk Kwan Nationals, 11-10-00 Hunter, NJ

2000: Attended:17th Ko Dan Ja Shim Sa, U.S.A. Carbondale, CO.

2000: Attended:1st Moments with the Masters (this is the first time "Moments with the Masters" was held at the same time as the Ko Dan Ja Shim Sa)

2000 October: Attended: 55th Anniversary Celebration of the Moo Duk Kwan. -Millennium visit to Seoul, Korea for Hwang Kee from World wide.

2001: Attended:23rd U.S. Soo Bahk Do (Tang Soo Do) Moo Duk Kwan Nationals, San Diego, CA

2001: Attended:18th Ko Dan Ja Shim Sa, U.S.A. West Copake, NY

2001: Attended: 2nd Moments with the Masters

2002 ***July 14th: Father / Founder: Hwang Kee passes away.***

2002 July 20th: The World Moo Duk Kwan and the Korean Soo Bahk Do Association called the special Board of Director's meeting for the new successor. Jin Mun Hwang (aka H. C. Hwang) became the 2nd Kwan Jang Nim for the Moo Duk Kwan.

2002 July 31st-August 3rd: Attended: The 24th U.S. Nationals at the Sheraton Hotel in East Rutherford, NJ. This National was contributed to memory of the Founder of the Moo Duk Kwan. The inaugural ceremony of the 2nd Kwan Jang Nim for the Moo Duk Kwan took placed.

2002 Attended:3rd Moments with the Masters
2002: Attended:1st Korean Ko Dan Ja Shim Sa
2002: Attended:19th Ko Dan Ja Shim Sa, U.S.A. Carbondale, CO

2003 July 21-25th: regional visit to the Cities of Manzanillo and Colima in the state of Colima and Guadalajara, Jalisco Mexico

2003: Attended:25th U.S. Soo Bahk Do (Tang Soo Do) Moo Duk Kwan Nationals, 8-1-03 East Rutherford, NJ

2003: Attended:,20th Ko Dan Ja Shim Sa, U.S.A., Camp Bethany, LA

2003: Attended:1st World Moo Duk Kwan Symposium, U.S.A. (hosting country)

2003: Attended:4th Moments with the Masters

2003: Kwan Jang Nim H.C. Hwang begins the World wide Vision Tour to relate Moo Duk Kwan History and Traditions. To share Objectives for the Moo Duk Kwan in the upcoming years.

Kwan Jang Nim's H.C. Hwangs motivation was as follows, "***Our beloved Founder of the Moo Duk Kwan, Grandmaster Hwang Kee passed away on July 14, 2002. Upon his passing, Grandmaster Hwang Kee became part of the Past. We are the present, and the future of the Moo Duk Kwan. It is dependant upon us and our actions. Now is a very important time in the Moo Duk Kwan's history for the present members to "Strengthen the foundation" of the Art so that the foundation will carry and ensure the future longevity of out art into the next generations***"

2003: December 12th**:** Attended: The PVT at Bradley, IL. (first time the tour was presented)

2003: February 8th: Attended: The PVT 1, at Bradley, IL (Region 5 and 7 together)

2004: Attended: 26th U.S. Soo Bahk Do (Tang Soo Do) Moo Duk Kwan Nationals, 8-20-04 San Diego, CA.

2004**:** Attended,21st Ko Dan Ja Shim Sa, U.S.A., Mobile, AL

2004: Attended:5th Moments with the Masters

2004: October 8th-15th Attended: Ko Dan Ja Shim Sa, Korea

2004: November, 12th-16th Attended and accompanied Kwan Jang Nim H.C. Hwang at the 2nd World Moo Duk Kwan Symposium held at the Hotel Resort, Villa Primavera, Guadalajara, Jalisco, Mexico

2005: August 24th-28th in Mexico visited: the Cities of Tuxtla Gutierrez and San Cristobal in the southern state of Chiapas to establish SBD MDK in that region

2005: September 30th-October 2nd: Attended: The 60th years of Moo Duk Kwan anniversary celebration in Sok Tcho, Kang Won Province, Korea.

2005: July 22nd: Kwan Jang Nim H.C. Hwang Appoints the 3rd Generation of U.S. TAC members.

They were; Sa Bom Nim's:

Steve Diaz (19461) – Neh Gong Bu

Frank Schermerhorn (19787)– Neh Gong Bu

Cash Cooper (23082) – Neh Gong Bu

Daymon Kenyon (19839) – Weh Gong Bu

Craig Hays (23132) – Weh Gong Bu

Jeff Griggs (23269) – Weh Gong Bu

Philip Bartolacci (20571) – Shim Gong Bu –Chairperson

Dae Kyu Jang (20780) – Shim Gong Bu

Ken Trevelyan (21909) – Shim Gong Bu

2005: July 23: Kwan Jang Nim H.C. Hwang forms the Hu Kyun In: Objective is to maintain, preserve, and perpetuate he History and Traditions of Soo Bahk Do Moo Duk Kwan, sharing it's knowledge, experience with its members and their community.

Members include: Sa Bom Nim's:

A. Robert Shipley, (#4825)

B. Hyuk Yoon Kwon, (#10805)

C. Ted Mason, (#12895)

D. Frank Bonsignore, (#15805)

F. Arthur Pryor, (#16505) 2005-2009

H. Jeffery Moonitz, (#17650)

I. Mary Ann Walsh, (#17926) Deceased: August 22nd , 2012

J. Wilton Bennett, (#19027)

Fred Messersmith, (#20729)

** 2009 Frank Schermerhorn,(#19787) added as liaison to T.A.C. (Technical, Advisory, Committee)

** 2012 Phillip Bartolacci, (20571) added

2005: Attended:27th U.S. Soo Bahk Do (Tang Soo Do) Moo Duk Kwan Nationals, 7-22-05 Orlando, FL

2005: Attended: 22nd Ko Dan Ja Shim Sa, U.S.A., Ramona, CA.

2005: Attended: 6th Moments with the Masters

2006: March 17th-18th: Attended:The Hu Kyun In's weekend (The first Guardians of the Art Seminars) at the Headquarters Do Jang in Springfield, NJ.

2006: April 25th- 28th in Mexico, accompanied Kwan Jang Nim H.C. Hwang to the city of Lagos de Moreno, Jalisco

2006: Attended:28th U.S. Soo Bahk Do (Tang Soo Do) Moo Duk Kwan Nationals, San Diego, CA

2006: Attended: 23rd Ko Dan Ja Shim Sa, U.S.A., Ramona, CA.

2006: Attended: 7th: Moments with the Masters

2007: January 26th–February 2nd: Attended: The PVT at the 25th U.S. Ko Dan Ja Shim Sa in Ramona, CA. Special sessions for Hwa Sun Hyung for SAC (Senior Advisory Committee member) and C Dan candidates.

2007: Attended:29th U.S. Soo Bahk Do (Tang Soo Do) Moo Duk Kwan Nationals, San Diego, CA

2007: Attended:24th Ko Dan Ja Shim Sa, U.S.A., Ramona, CA

2007: Attended: 8th Moments with the Masters

2008: Attended:30th U.S. Soo Bahk Do (Tang Soo Do) Moo Duk Kwan Nationals, San Diego, CA

2008: Attended: 25th Ko Dan Ja Shim Sa, U.S.A., Ramona, CA

2008: Promoted to 9th Dan (Under Kwan Jang Nim H.C. Hwang)

2008: Attended: 9th Moments with the Masters

2009: April 17th:Kwan Jang Nim visit's Region 5 for Nai Han Ji Hyung clinic with attended Ko Dan Ja.

2009: Attended: 10th: Moments with the Masters

2009: Attended: 31st U.S. Soo Bahk Do (Tang Soo Do) Moo Duk Kwan Nationals, San Diego, Ca.

2009: Attended,26th Ko Dan Ja Shim Sa, U.S.A., Ramona, CA

2010: February 18th-20th: Attended the U.S. SAC (Senior Advisory Committee) training and meeting at Santa Inez, CA.

They were: W.Y. Chung Sa Bom Nim (410), Kwan Jang Nim H.C. Hwang (509), L. Seiberlich Sa Bom Nim (1815), **Russ Hanke (4137) Sa Bom Nim,** and V. Martinov (10189) Sa Bom

2010: March 13th-14th Instructed: Moo Pahl Dan Khum in Mexico City

2010: Attended:11th: Moments with the Masters

2010: Attended ,27th Ko Dan Ja Shim Sa, U.S.A., Ramona, CA

2010: Attended:32nd U.S. Soo Bahk Do (Tang Soo Do) Moo Duk Kwan Nationals, Cherry Hill, NJ

2011 May 4th: Kwan Jang Nim H.C. Hwang conducted the U.S. SAC (Senior Advisory Committee) Tele Conference for the "START (Share The ART)" program.

2011: Attended:10th Moments with the Masters

2011: Attended: 28th Ko Dan Ja Shim Sa, U.S.A., Ramona, CA

2011: Attended: 33rd U.S. Soo Bahk Do (Tang Soo Do) Moo Duk Kwan Nationals, San Diego, CA

2011: June 1st: Kwan Jang Nim appointed the 4th Generation of the U.S. T.A.C.
They were: Sa Bom Nim's:
Cash Cooper (23082 - Chairman
Bill Nelson (21420) – Neh Gong Bu
Lisa Kozak (23540) – Neh Gong Bu
Josh Lockwood (29755) – Neh Gong Bu
Daymon Kenyon (19839) – Weh Gong Bu
Craig Hays (23132) – Weh Gong Bu
Jeff Griggs (23269) – Weh Gong Bu
Kris Poole (20632) – Shim Gong Bu
Dae Kyu Jang (20780) – Shim Gong Bu
Jennifer Gibbons (32238) – Shim Gong Bu

2011: June 1st: Kwan Jang Nim conducted a Tele-Conference for promoting the "START" program. The U.S. HKI (Hu Kyun In), TAC (Technical Advisory Committee). BOD (Board of Directors), and NPVT (National PVT Committee) were attended the conference.

2012: Attended: 12th Moments with the Masters

2012 April 13th-15th: Kwan Jang Nim attended the Region 5 Dan Shim Sa and clinics at Merrillville, IN.

2012: Attended: ,29th Ko Dan Ja Shim Sa, U.S.A., Ramona, CA.

2012: Attended: 34th U.S. Soo Bahk Do (Tang Soo Do) Moo Duk Kwan Nationals, Cherry Hill, NJ

2013: Attended:12th Moments with the Masters

2013: Attended,30th Ko Dan Ja Shim Sa, U.S.A., Ramona, CA.
2013: Attended: 35th U.S. Soo Bahk Do (Tang Soo Do) Moo Duk Kwan Nationals,

2014: Attended:14th Moments with the Masters

2014 : Attended:31st Ko Dan Ja Shim Sa, USA, Ramona, CA. November 14th-21st

2014: Attended:36th U.S. Soo Bahk Do (Tang Soo Do) Moo Duk Kwan Nationals, Salt Lake City, UT

2015: Closes Wyandotte, MI. Dojang to continue to serve the Kwan Jang Nim as Senior Advisory Committee member, and focus on the Five Levels of "The Mind Training Praxis" as explained in the "Moo Do Chul Hahk "

(We have included the Region 5 Championships and Dan Shims Sa he attended from this point on.) * highlighted areas to be checked

2015: March 7th: Attended 7th Dan and Up training session at the HQ Dojang in Springfield, NJ
2015: Attended: Region 5 Championship / 139th Dan Shim Sa and clinics, Merrillville, IN.
2015: July 30th – August 2nd: attended 37th U.S. National Festival, Garden Grove, Ca.
2015: October 30th – November 1st: attended World Moo Duk Kwan 70th anniversary celebration in Suwon, South Korea
2015: Attended: Region 5 140th Dan Shim Sa and clinics at Merrillville, IN.

2015: November 13th- 15th: Attended 15th Moment with the Masters, Ramona, Ca.

2015: November 13th – 20th: Conducted 32nd U.S. Ko Dan Ja Shim Sa, Ramona, Ca.

2016: Attended: Region 5 Championship / 141st Dan Shim Sa and clinics at Merrillville, IN.
2016: June 29th – July3rd: Attended the 38th U.S. National Festival, Anaheim, Ca.
2016: Attended: Region 5 142nd Dan Shim Sa and clinics at Merrillville, IN.
2016: November 11th – 13th: Attended the 16th USA Moment with the Masters, Ramona, Ca.
2016: November 11th – 18th: Attended the 33rd U.S. Ko Dan Ja Shim Sa, Ramona, Ca.

2017: Attended: Region 5 Dan Shim Sa Championship and clinics at Pheasant Run, IL.
2017: August 10th- 12th Attended the 39th U.S. National Festival, Montgomery ,TX.
2017: Attended: Region 5 143rd Dan Shim Sa and clinics at Chebanse, IL.
2017: November 10th – 12th : Attended the 17th Moment with the Masters, Montgomery TX.
2017: November 10th – 17th: Attended the 34th USA Ko Dan Ja Shim Sa, Montgomery, TX.

2018: March 23-25: Attended the Region 5 Championship / 141st Dan Shim Sa and the TAC tour in Illinois.
2018: August 9th -12th: Attended the 40th U.S. Nationals Festival & World Moo Duk Kwan 12th Designees Zone Symposium, Houston, TX
2018: Attended: Region 5 142nd Dan Shim Sa and clinics at Marquette, MI
2018: November 9th – 11th: Attended the 18th Moment with the Masters, Houston, TX
2018: November 9th -16th: Attended the U.S.A. 35th Ko Dan Ja Shim Sa, Houston. TX

2019: Attended the Region 5 Championship / 143rd Dan Shim Sa, Pheasant Run, IL.
2019: July 25th-27th: Attended the 41st U.S. Nationals Festival, Portland, Oregon
2019: Attended the Region 5 144th Dan Shim Sa and clinics, Marquette, Mi.
(He taught the clinic to the membership on the connection of breathing and technique, this would be the last clinic he taught to the membership of region 5)
2019: November 8th-10th, attended the U.S. 19th Moment with the Masters, Midway, Utah
2019: November 8th- 15th, attended the U.S.A. 36th Ko Dan Ja Shim Sa, Midway, Utah

2020: January 8th: Sa Bom Nim passes away in his sleep.

Sa Bom Nim Hanke's students who obtained Ko Dan Ja levels:
Kendall Jenkins, (Dan Bon: 14219), George Manns,(Dan Bon: 14718) Paul Barton,(Dan Bon: 17409, *deceased, 2002*), Robert Howell,(Dan Bon 18409),David Beiermann,(Dan Bon: 19442,deceased 2013),Susan Robins,(Dan Bon: 19459), Steven Diaz,(Dan Bon: 19461), Mark Wilson(Dan Bon: 21360,deceased 2011), Glenda Sheets,(Dan Bon: 22671),Lisa Donnelly,(Dan Bon: 23279),Steven Lemner, (Dan Bon: 23703), Jane Kaufman,(Dan Bon: 26108),David Broughton,(Dan Bon: 26229), Mon Faulk (Dan Bon: 26298),Robert Preville,(Dan Bon: 27665), Joey LaJoice (Dan Bon: 29422), Josh Lockwood,(Dan Bon: 29775), Joyce Tredeau,(Dan Bon: 29984), Michael Zickafoose,(Dan Bon: 30699),William Parrish,(Dan Bon: 31209), Kenny Swaffer,(Dan Bon: 35156), Ron Strong,(Dan Bon: 37352), Carl Vonck, (Dan Bon: 39474)

**Note the time line does not include all the clinics at his students Dojang's he conducted throughout the U.S.A. and all the Regional, National and International Dan Shim Sa's, Tournaments , summer camps that he attended also over his lifetime. We thank him for his years of service, leadership and dedication to the Kwan Jang Nim, membership and art. His memory and energy will live on through the members who's lives he touch by his living example of the art in action.

Steven Lemner's History:

Master Paul Barton
17409

Steven Lemner began his training in 1981, at the Kankakee Y.M.C.A., under the direction of Master Paul Barton (Dan Bon, 17409).

Tested for Gup ranks:
10th-7th Gup, 11/24/1981
7th-5th Gup, 3/2/1982
4th Gup, 8/3/1982
3rd Gup, 12/16/1982
2nd Gup, 7/11/1983
1st Gup, 12/7/1983

Dan testing ranks:
Tested for: Chodan (1st Degree) 5/29/1984
Tested for: Edan Dan (2nd Degree) 10/20/1987
Tested for: Kyo-Sa (Certified instructor) 4/5/1988
Tested for: Sam Dan (3rd Degree),11/10/1990
Attended the 10th U.S. Ko Dan Ja Shim Sa at the Headquarters Do Jang in Springfield
The last time the Founder, Hwang Kee was present in the U.S.A.
Sa Dan (4th Degree), 12/15/1994
Sa Bom (Master Instructor) 12/15/1994
Tested for: O Dan (5th Degree) Attended the 18th U.S. Ko Dan Ja Shim Sa in Carbondale, CO. 7/10/2000
Tested for: Yuk Dan (6th Degree) Attended the 25th U.S. Ko Dan Ja Shim Sa in Ramona, CA. 2/2/2007
Tested for: Chil Dan (7th Degree) Attended the 31st Ko Dan Ja Shim Sa, USA, Ramona, CA. 11/21/2014
Attended the 32nd U.S. Ko Dan Ja Shim Sa, Ramona, Ca., 2015 November 13th – 20th, Guest

His whole family has also trained:
His wife Darci Lemner (Dan Bon, 46642)
Son's Aaron Lemner (Dan Bon, 31890) Craig Lemner (Dan Bon, 41009),
Daughter, Jessica (Lemner) Fancher (Dan Bon, 41004)
Son-in-law Adam Fancher (Dan Bon, 31891)
and step son Mitchell Goodknecht (Dan Bon, 46001)

Sa Bom Nim Lemners opened his Dojang and began teaching in 1986.
He has trained 178 Dan Members

7 Ko Dan Ja, 10 Kyo-Sa's, 15 Jo-Kyo's.

He began training with Sa Bom Nim Russ Hanke (Dan Bon, 4137) in 1986.

He attended the Soo Bahk Do® (Tang Soo Do) Moo Duk Kwan® 50th anniversary celebration in Seoul, Korea in 1995, and was chosen to be the stage director for the event.

He has held the position on Regional P.V.T. (Presidents / Vision / Tour) Director for Region 5, and has been a member of the National P.V.T board from it's conception in 1993.

He has attended nationals in Florida, Texas, Ohio and California.
He was a Region 5 Fighting team member for Nationals in Texas.

He developed and has operated the Bourbonnais Park District Martial Arts program since 1987, and was chosen as volunteer of the year by the Chamber of Commerce in 2010.

He has been a surgical technician at Riverside Medical Center since 1978, and is in charge of the Robotics program.

He oversees the Region 5, Kwan Jang Nim H.C. Hwang and World Moo Duk Kwan Facebook page's.

He has written the history timeline for the Founder Hwang Kee, Kwan Jang Nim H.C. Hwang and Sa Bom Nim Russ Hanke to preserve it's history and tradition.

He enjoys, music, cooking, travel, reading, weapons training, photography and spending time with family and friends. He has 4 grandchildren, Dakota, Cheyenne, Chloe, Josie.

www.ingramcontent.com/pod-product-compliance
Ingram Content Group UK Ltd.
Pitfield, Milton Keynes, MK11 3LW, UK
UKHW050147280726
14058UKWH00007B/887

9 781794 739253